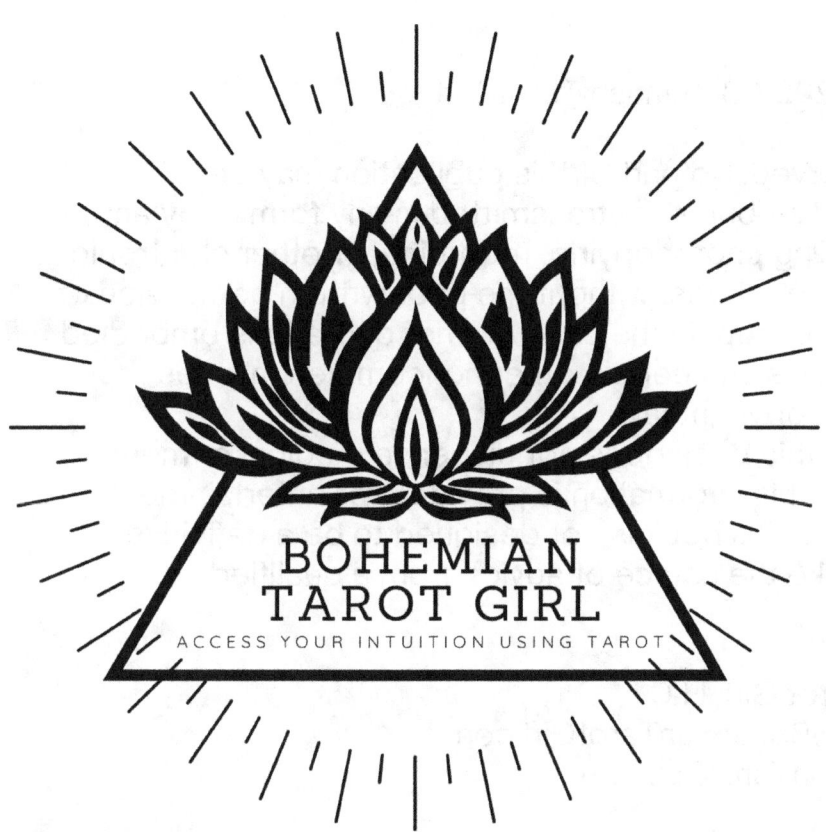

BOHEMIAN
TAROT GIRL
ACCESS YOUR INTUITION USING TAROT

Bohemian Tarot Girl, LLC
Email: Team@BohemianTarotGirl.com
www.BohemianTarotGirl.com

Paperback# 978-0-578-26100-3

TABLE OF CONTENTS

TABLE OF CONTENTS
CONTINUED

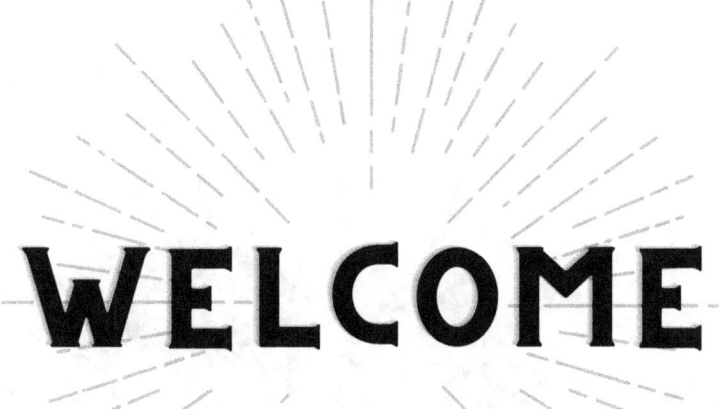

WELCOME

Welcome to the Wandering Traveler Tarot coloring book! Learn about Tarot cards and get connected with their meanings while doing a relaxing coloring activity. The images in this coloring book are from the Bohemian Tarot Girl's Wandering Traveler Tarot Deck. The cards have been converted so you may color them in and add your own interpretation.

Coloring is a great form of relaxation and can get you into a meditative state, in which you are uniquely positioned to be more open and ready to access your intuition. I hope you enjoy this coloring book, and please stay connected at www.BohemianTarotGirl.com to learn more about tarot!

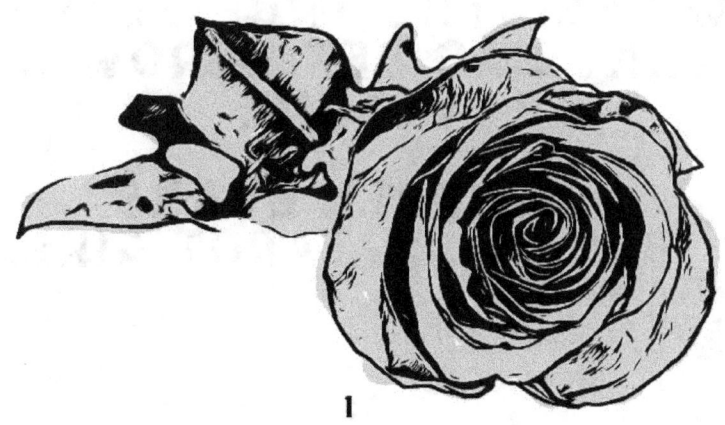

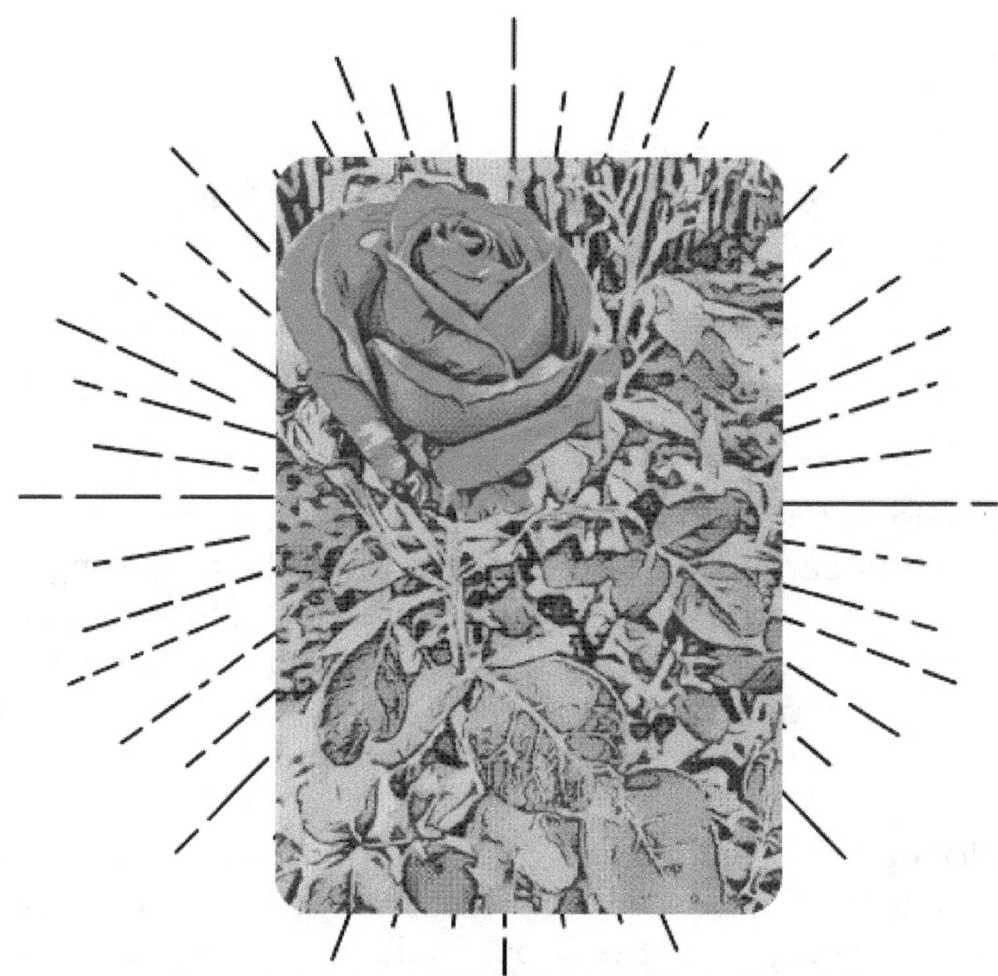

ROSES REMIND ME THAT
WHEN WE USE OUR
INTUITION WE BLOOM, AND
WE SEE THE TRUE BEAUTY
THAT HAS BEEN GROWING
WITHIN.

-KENDALL EVANS
BOHEMIAN TAROT GIRL

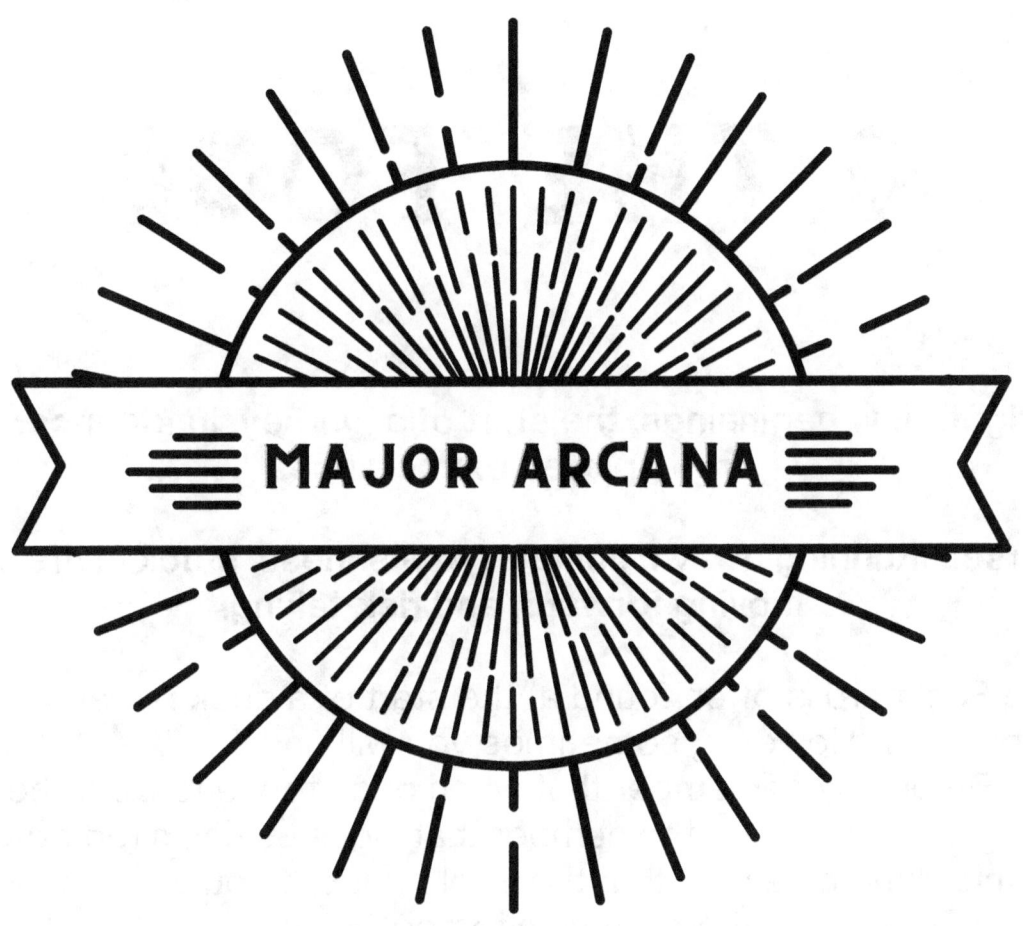

MAJOR ARCANA

0. THE FOOL

Upright: New beginnings, the start of a journey, innocence, and free-spirited exuberance.

Reversed: Running away from fate, foolishness, stuck in life or not moving forward, and risk-taking.

The Fool card is often found at the start of a deck because it is number zero. However, sometimes you will find it at the end of the deck. Either way, remember that when one story ends, another one will begin again. Zero is the number that signifies unlimited potential, and this is the message that the Fool brings. If you start a journey, there is unlimited potential.

About the Image on the Card
We start the journey in a small beach town called Ilwaco, Washington, at Cape Disappointment. This beautiful park lets you see where the Columbia River meets the Pacific Ocean. This photo reminds me of the adventure ahead, and what it's like to stand in quiet and see the beauty of the unknown.

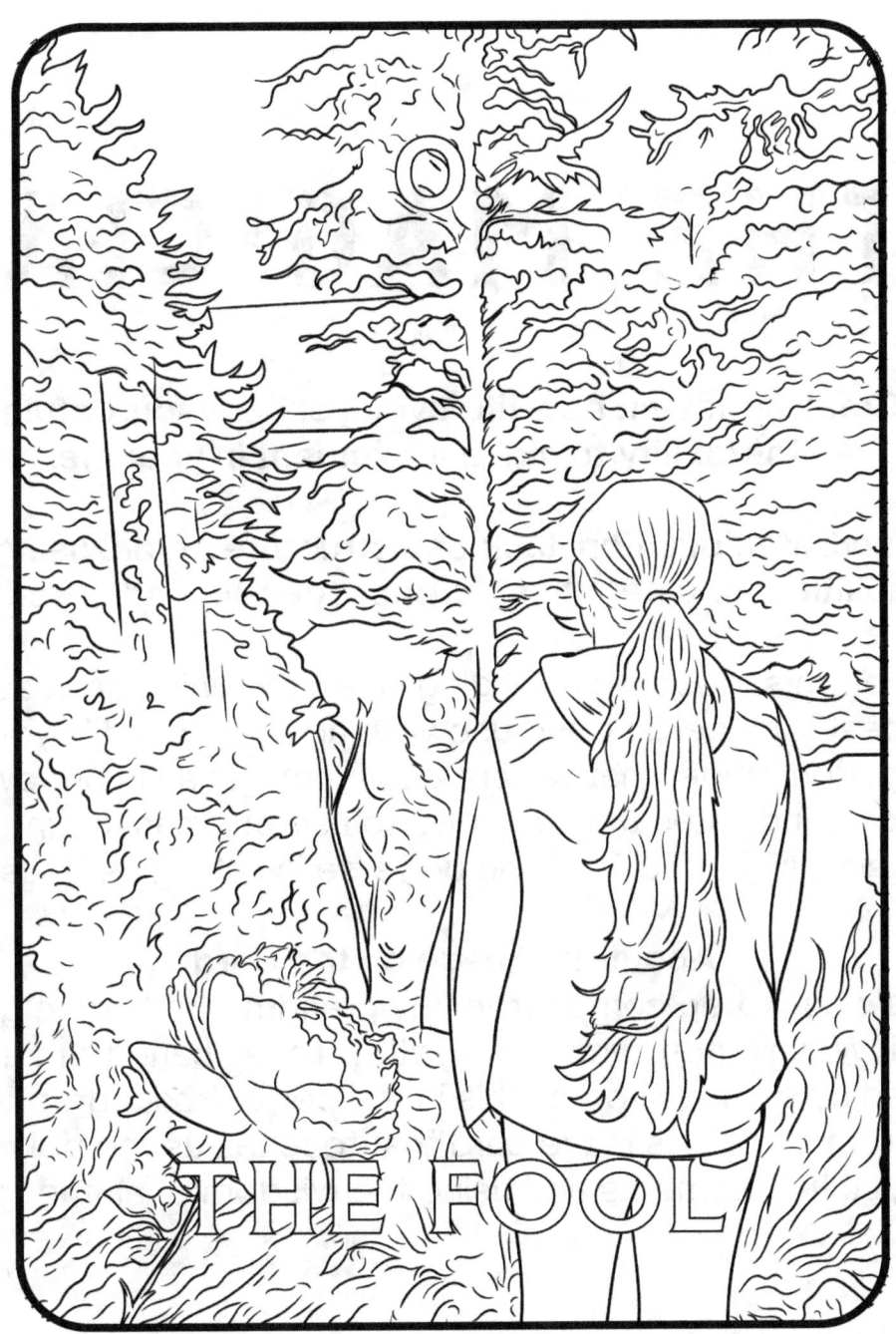

I. THE MAGICIAN

Upright: Creative power, new life cycle, skill, resourcefulness, and action/ability to make movement in your life.

Reversed: Manipulation, lack of a structured plan, using your abilities for a negative purpose, deceit, and greed.

This card often surfaces in a reading when the universe is asking you to manifest your desires and use your abilities to aid in your life's creations. Remember that we are each a magician in our own lives, and this card indicates that we need to use our manifesting abilities to gain insight into what the universe is asking us to seek.

About the Image on the Card

This card's backdrop comes from my grandmother's rose garden in Kirkland, Washington, where the yellow roses hang from an arbor backed by a tranquil pool. This is the perfect backdrop to the Magician card. This is the card that teaches us the power of mastering all the elements and using the wisdom of all the tarot suits.

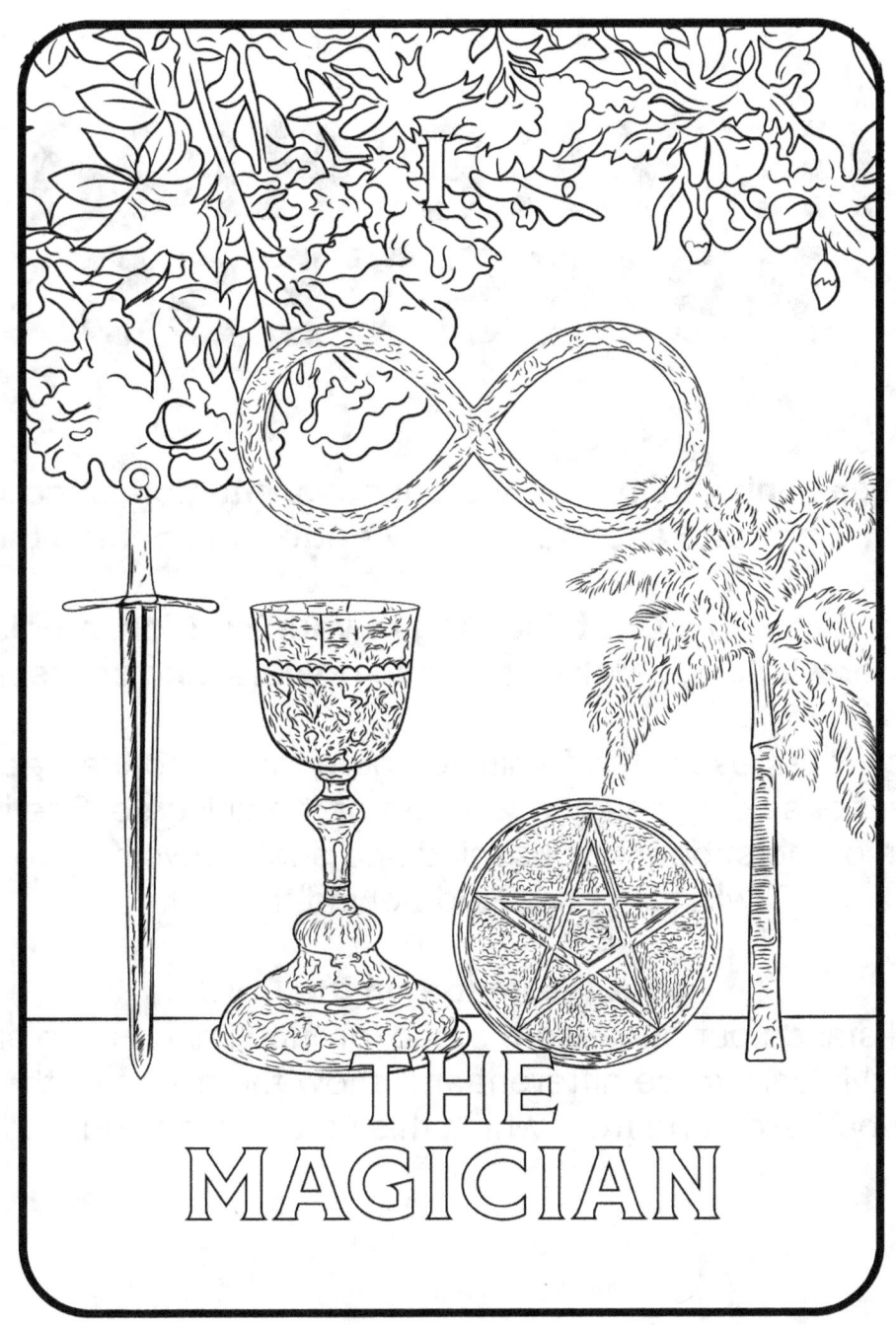

II. THE HIGH PRIESTESS

Upright: Femininity, higher consciousness, intuition, subconscious mind, wisdom, and access to knowledge from behind the veil.

Reversed: Repression, not listening to your intuition, blocking your inner wisdom, blocked psychic powers, and secrets.

The High Priestess is the feminine figure that is connected to her higher consciousness, the wisdom of the universe. She is the guardian of the subconscious mind and she knows how to access what is concealed behind the veil.

About the Image on the Card

This card stands out because the background image is so abstract. I wanted this card to be different and show the magic of the child's superhero cape from which this picture was sourced.

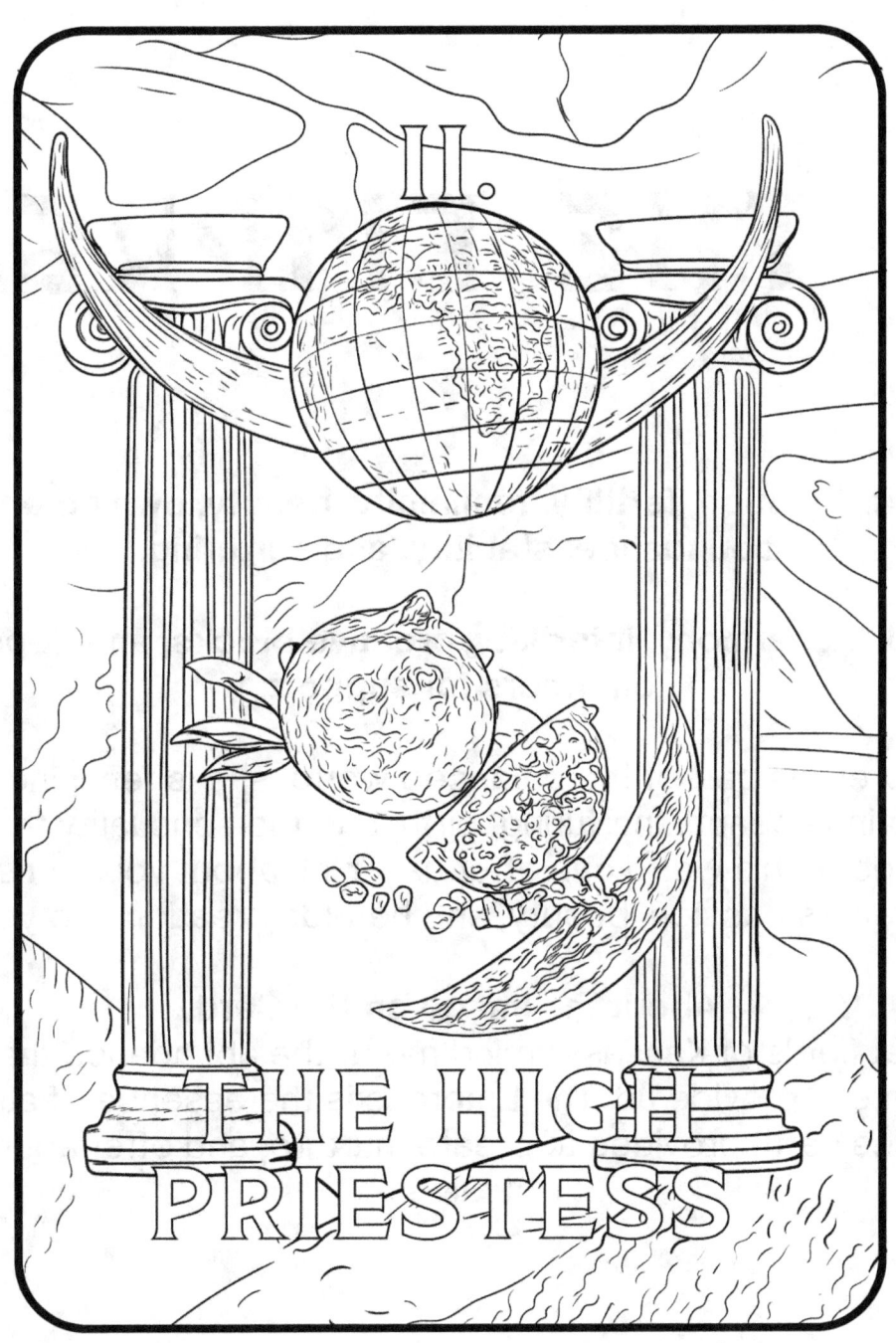

III. THE EMPRESS

Upright: Creation, fertility, femininity, beauty, owning oneself, abundance, stability, and nurturing.

Reversed: Disharmony, infertility, creative blocks, and dependence on others for support.

The Empress is part of the balanced world; she is feminine energy. She brings beauty, nurturing, birth, and the sensuality that the pleasures of this world can offer us. Think about your senses and what creates passion, beauty, and heralds creation into your life.

About the Image on the Card
The wheat fields of Kansas remind me of the abundance that mother earth can provide us. The Empress is the essence of all the possibilities earth provides to create, nurture, and offer abundance in our lives.

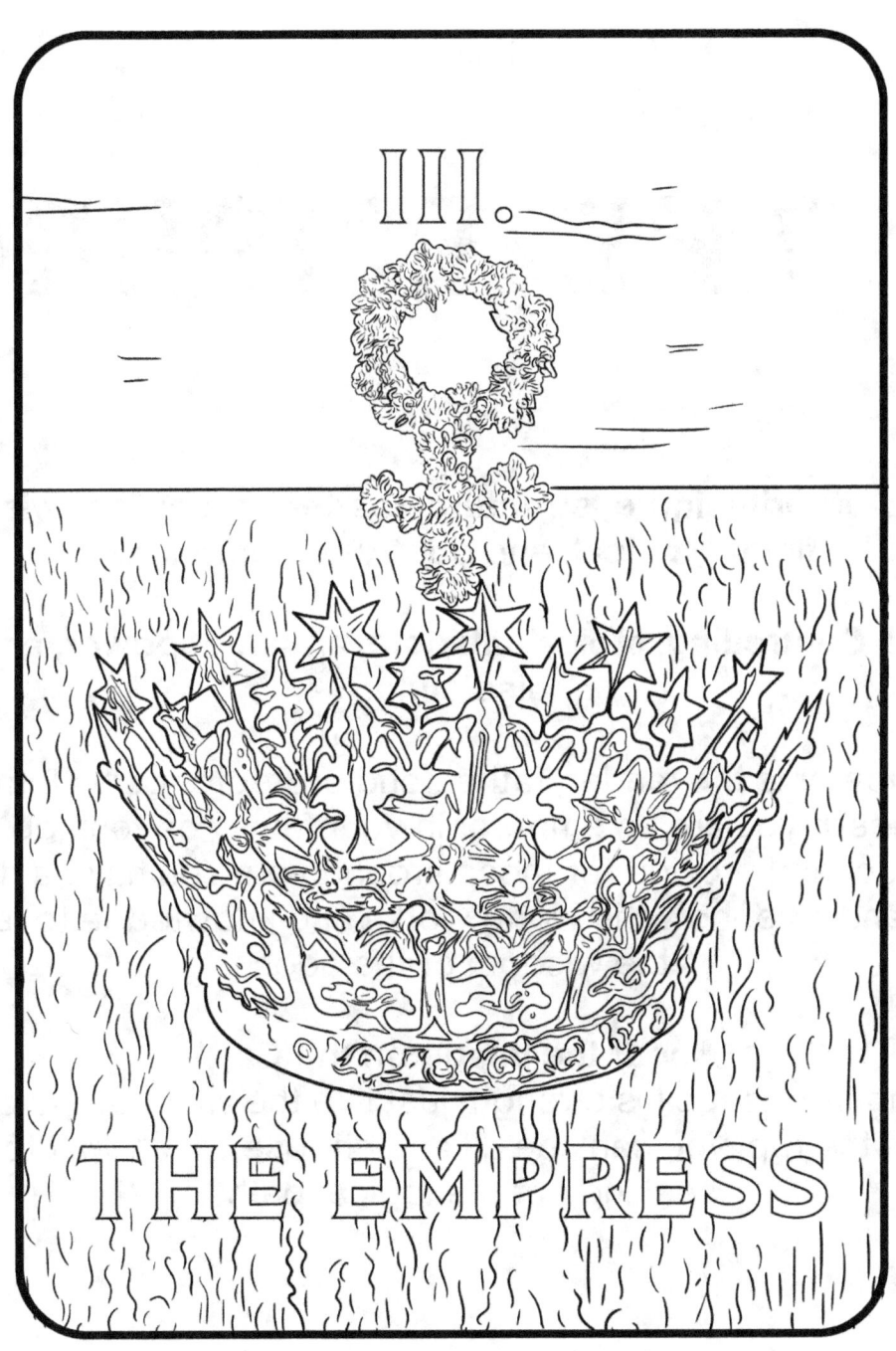

IV. THE EMPEROR

Upright: Authority figure, structure, leader, masculine, wise father figure, logical, and controlled emotions.

Reversed: Controlling, stoic, inflexible, abuse of power, and lack of discipline.

The Emperor is the leader, father, and protector of his family and loved ones. If you are an emperor in your family or your job, you will protect and provide for those around you. You have a deep understanding of how the world works and knowledge to lead with the wisdom of the ages.

About the Image on the Card
The Emperor keeps his strength just like the walls of the canyon. Here at the top, you can see all and choose which way to go by seeking out the logical paths.

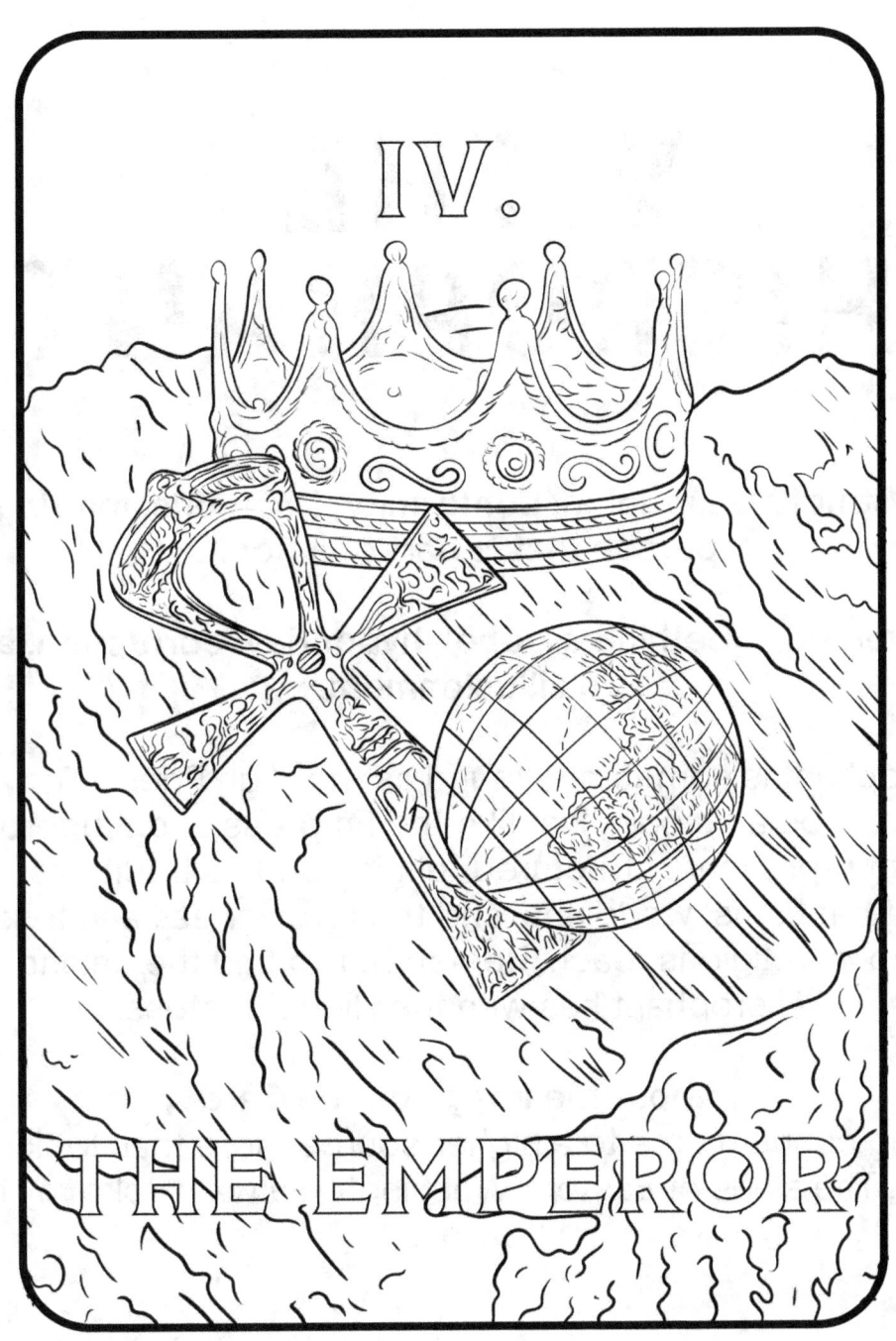

V. THE HIEROPHANT

Upright: Structured religion, conformity, traditions, marriage, and a person that is part of a flock.

Reversed: Freethinker, rebel, hypocrisy, corruption, and disillusionment.

The Hierophant is sometimes found as the High Priest. They are two sides of the same coin, just like the Empress and Emperor. The Hierophant represents structured religion and its traditions. This card speaks of baptisms, weddings, and the forgiveness and lessons that the traditional religions teach. Remember to find the balance that the Hierophant has with the High Priestess.

About the Image on the Card
Nothing connects me to a higher source more than looking at a sunset. The skies of Eastern Washington always take my breath away.

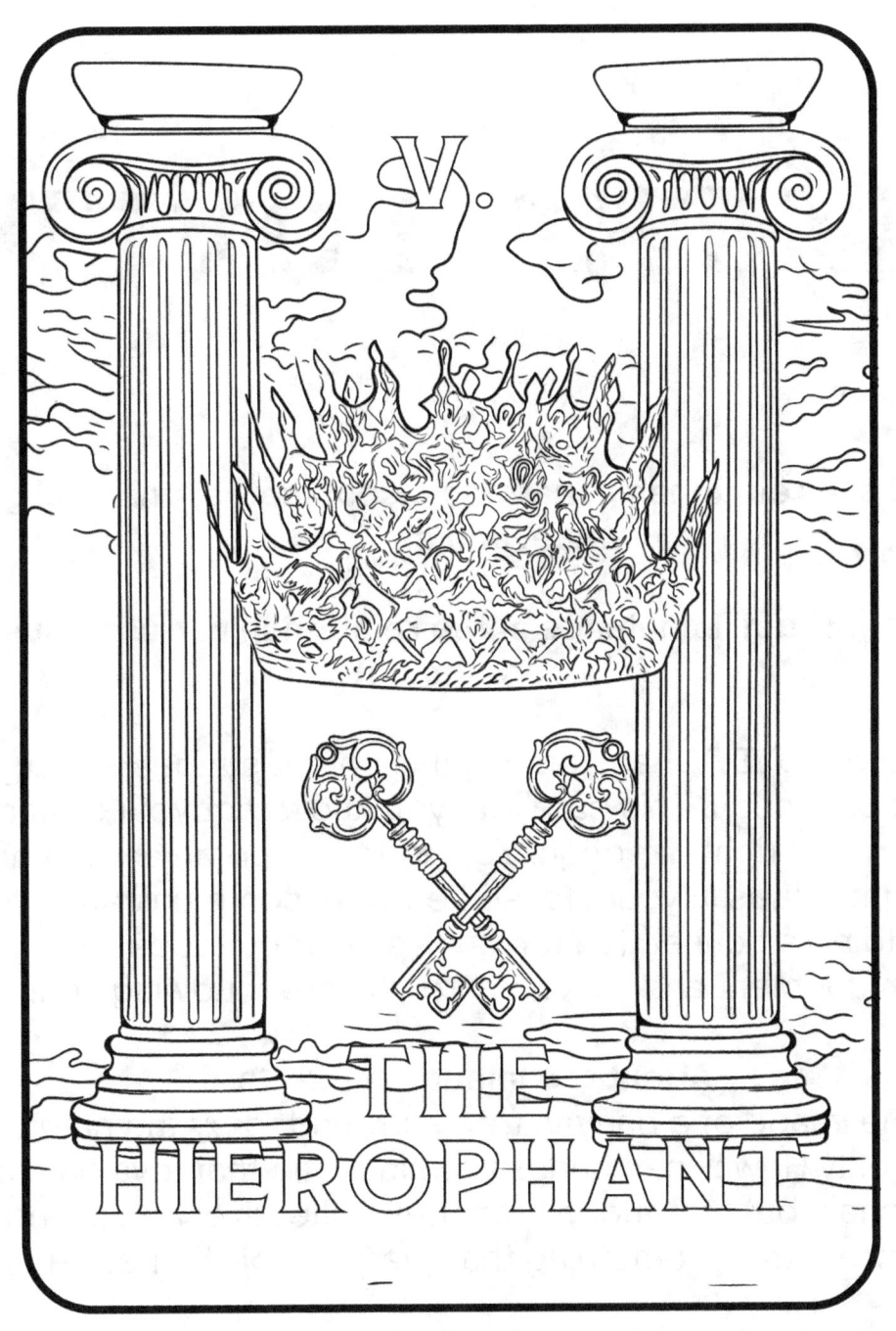

VI. THE LOVERS

Upright: Love relationship, harmony, soul mates, union, alignment in value, and choices.

Reversed: Lust, imbalance in the relationship, trust issues, and detachment.

The card of LOVE. When you pull this card it suggests that you have a deep connection. This card lets you know that your relationship is heading in the right direction. You and this person are connected in all the right values in your life, so keep the communication going and this could be a connection for life. It's all about accessing your own higher judgment and making sure you are following your heart.

About the Image on the Card
This is the image of a banyan tree surrounded by the natural beauty that only Hawaii can bring. It reminds me that love has many branches, but that those branches collectively build and give strength to something that reaches for the heavens.

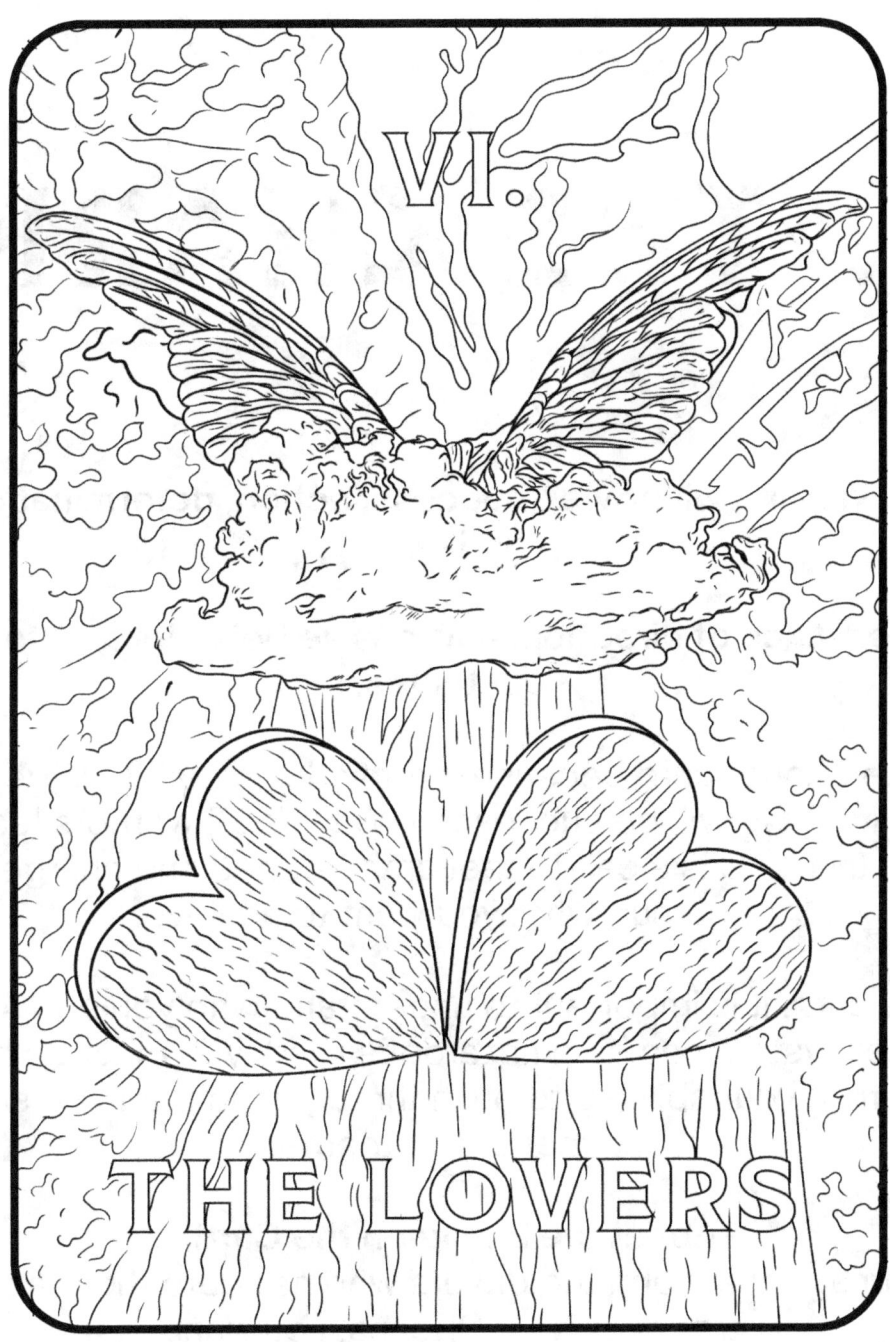

VII. THE CHARIOT

Upright: Victory, willpower, success, action, determination, and drive.

Reversed: Lack of direction, aggressive behaviors, defeat, and obstacles.

I love the Chariot card because it reminds us that if we get in and drive our lives, we will be successful. We are all warriors leading our lives, and this card is a call to feel emboldened and charge forward to pursue what you want to achieve.

With this card, it is important to understand who you are. Although your belief system can be a hazardous road, you must be bold and confident in your abilities to push through and lead yourself to a successful outcome.

About the Image on the Card
The carriage team and the drivers who navigate the crazy, wild streets of New Orleans, Louisiana.

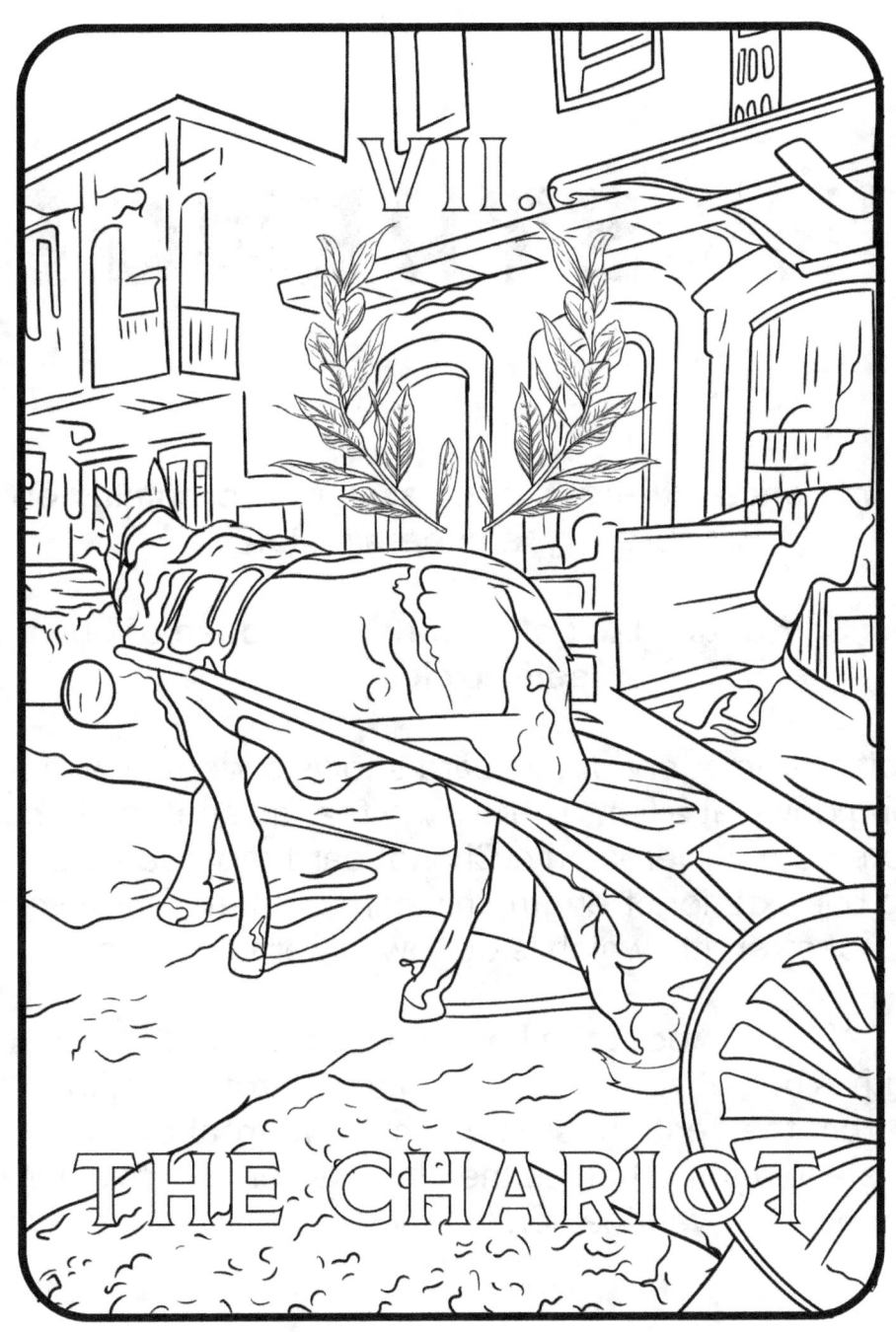

VIII. STRENGTH

Upright: Influence, strength, compassion, overcoming obstacles, bravery, and persuasion.

Reversed: Self-doubt, lack of confidence, abuse of power, and no self-discipline.

The traditional imagery of this card shows a woman with a serene face gazing down at a lion. There is no fear as she gently coaxes the lion to surrender. Whereas the Chariot card represents the strength of will and our exterior strength, this card is what is really at the heart of strength, which is our own internal strength.

About the Image on the Card

Strength is not all about force or who is stronger. Real strength comes from the gentleness with which we treat others. Love and understanding of others is the ultimate force in this universe. Sometimes even the lion (scary cat) needs to be loved.

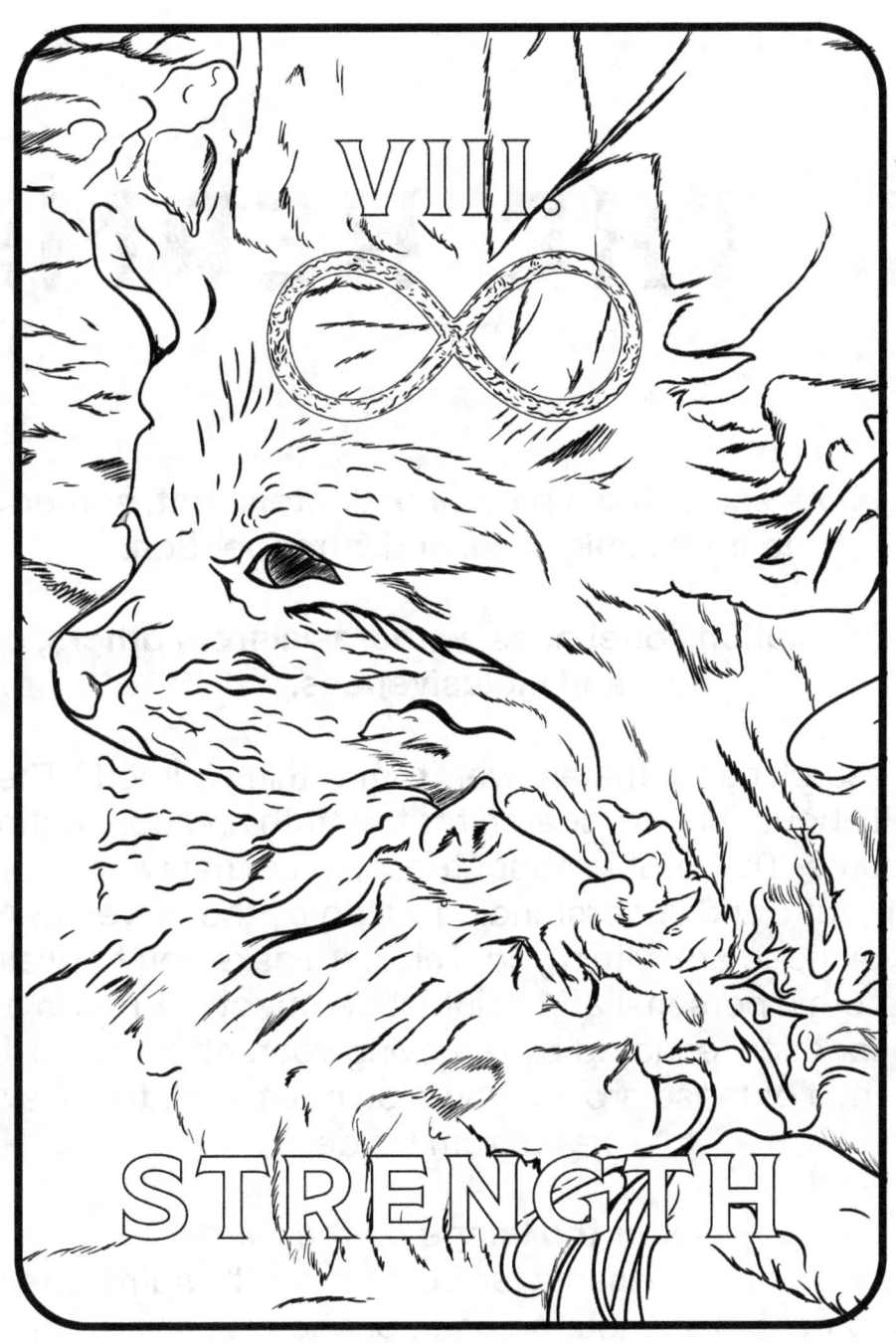

IX. THE HERMIT

Upright: Soul searching, spiritual enlightenment, solitude, lone journey, guidance, and introspection.

Reversed: Isolation, loneliness, withdrawal from others, paranoia, and inclusiveness.

Are you searching for the answer from within yourself? The Hermit card is all about our own search for the truth and connection to our higher source. The tarot is about teaching us that we all contain the power, truth, and understanding willed by the universe. All the answers you need are within you. This card asks you to evaluate your life from both a personal and spiritual perspective. This is a time for self-introspection, enacted by removing yourself from the judgment and influence of those around you. You must seek the answers you need from inside.

About the Image on the Card
The journey is not necessarily far from home. It's sometimes found in the forest behind your home in Snohomish, Washington.

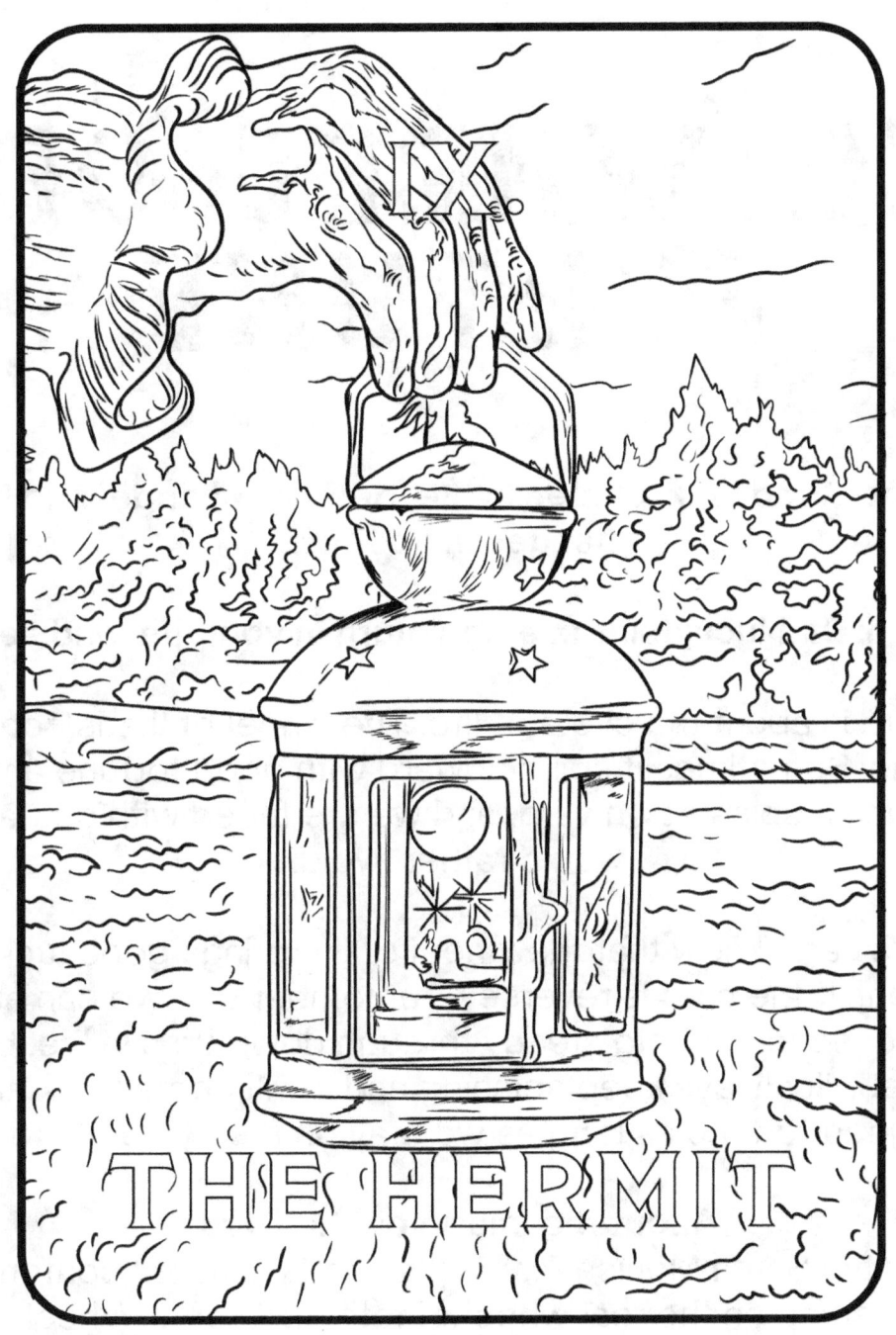

X. WHEEL OF FORTUNE

Upright: Good luck, cycles in life, destiny, change, and happy changes in your life.

Reversed: Bad luck, failure, a downturn in your life, and setbacks.

This card is about the cycle of life. The wheel of life is constantly spinning. Sometimes it spins upward with good fortune and luck. Sometimes it spins downward, and we are faced with obstacles we would rather avoid.

With this card, know that the wheel of life brings good luck at this moment. If the card is reversed, remember that we can always change direction or hold steady through downturns in life, because the wheel will always keep spinning and it will come back around to good fortune as long as we stay on the cycle of life.

About the Image on the Card
A day at the Santa Monica Pier in California, where I contemplated getting on the real wheel of fate, the Ferris Wheel.

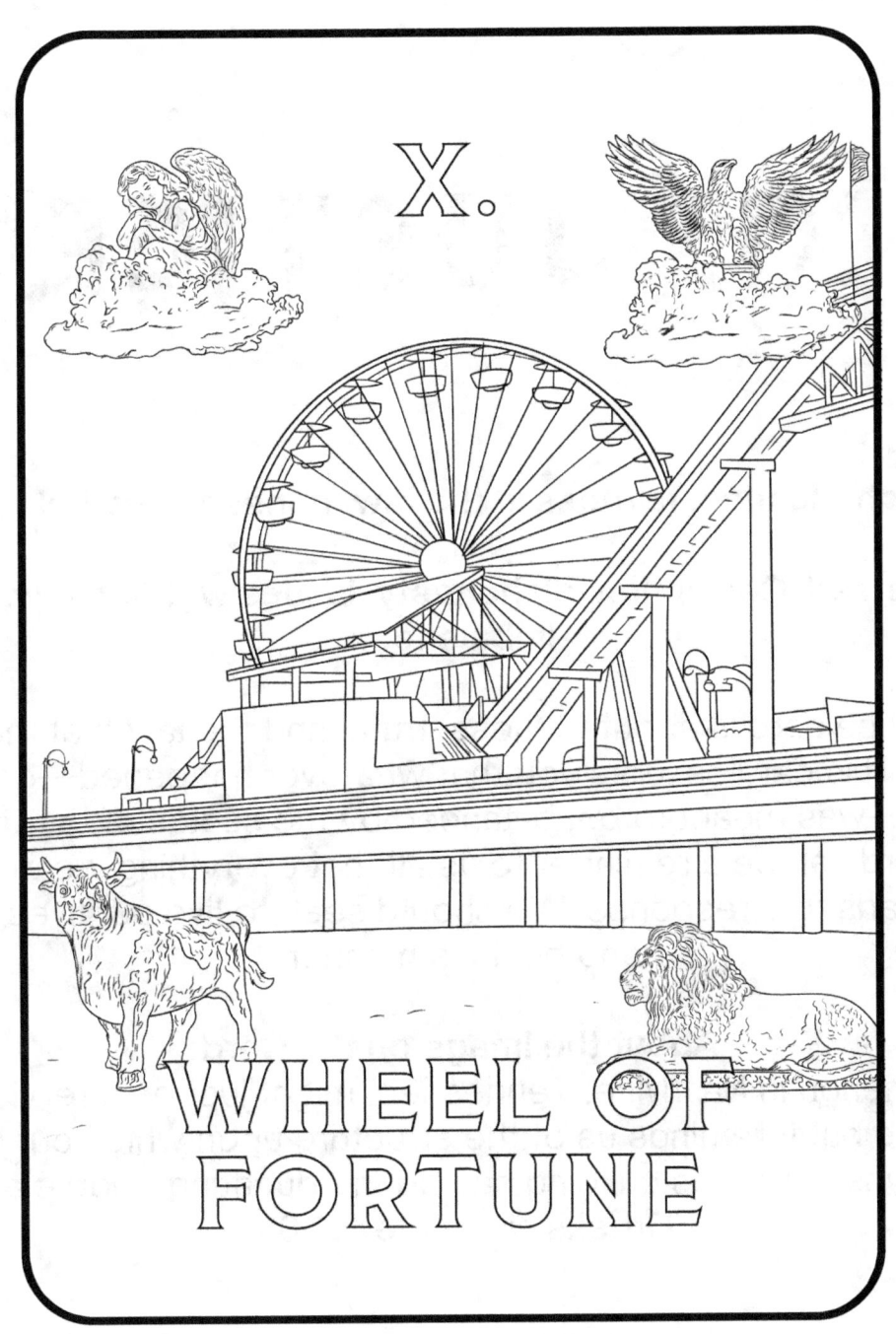

X.

WHEEL OF
FORTUNE

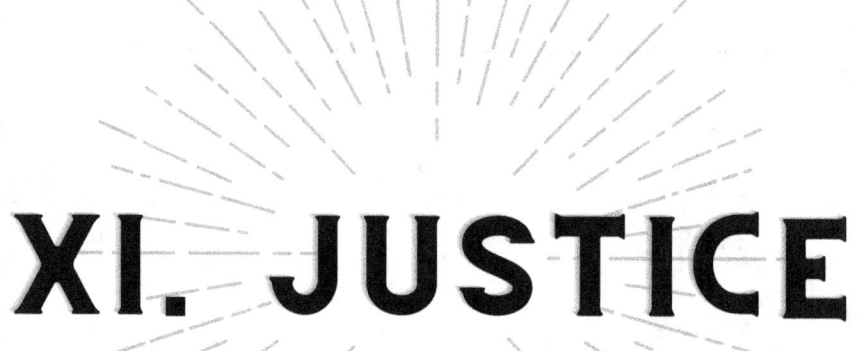

XI. JUSTICE

Upright: Justice, fairness in the law, honesty, and balance.

Reversed: Corruption, dishonesty, issues with the law, and imbalance.

The Justice card is about fairness, truth, and the law that maintains balance. This card assures you that whatever happened—or is yet to happen—was meant to be, balanced by the scales of the universe. This card can be a reminder to us all that everything we do in this world leads to a response. We should seek to live our lives in a just and positive manner.

About the Image on the Card
The Parthenon in Nashville, Tennessee, might just be a replica of the real one but it reminds us of the structure upon which our justice system was built. This building has been educating people about the Greeks since the 1930s.

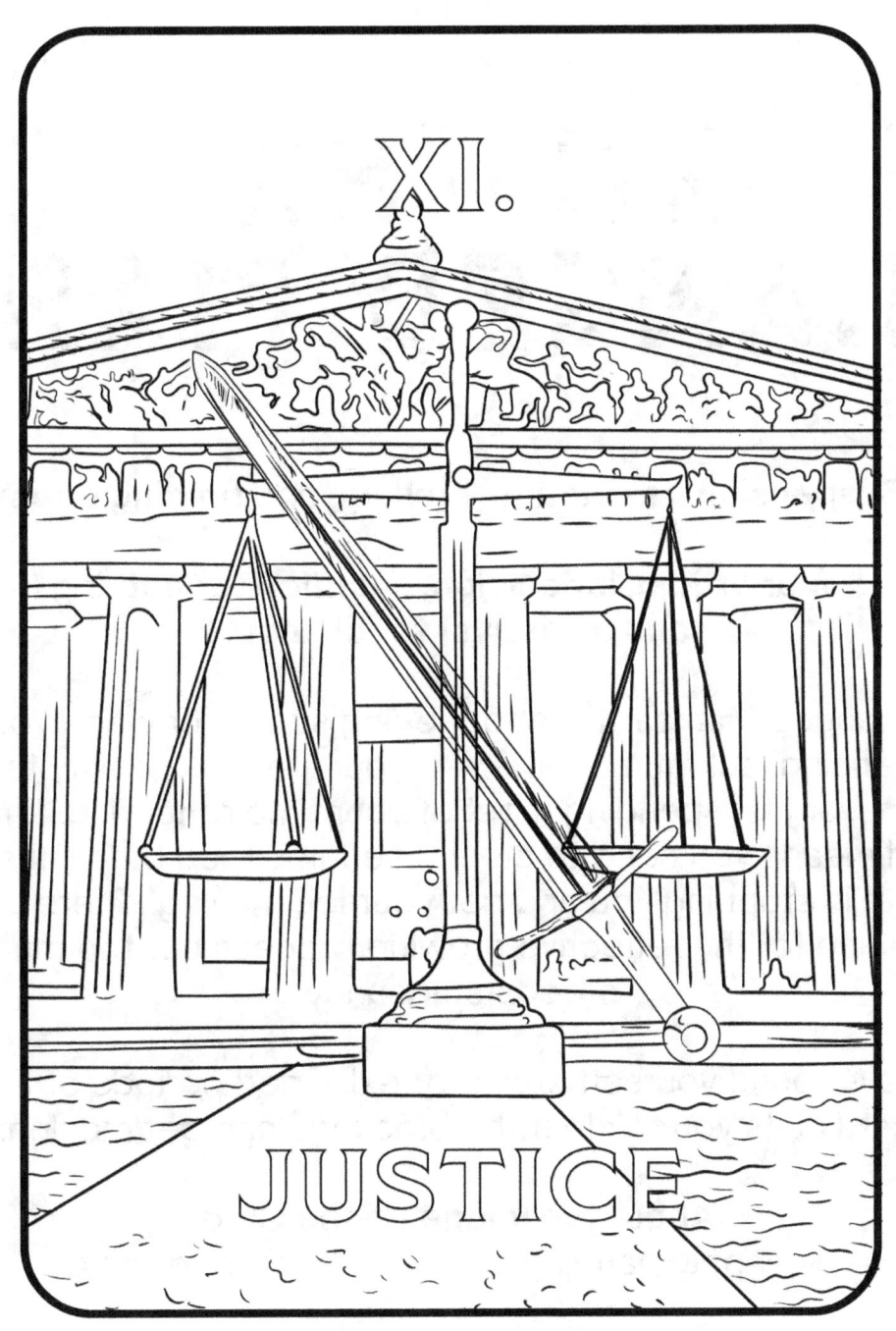

XII. THE HANGED MAN

Upright: Suspension, restriction, stalling, and holding oneself back.

Reversed: Martyrdom, indecision, sacrifice for nothing in return, and a catalyst for change.

The Hanged Man card is about being stuck, for when you are experiencing lack of movement in your life, the inability to make decisions, or just spending most of your time reflecting. Know that this card means you need to clear a self-imposed block. It's time to find what is stopping you and get yourself moving. There is a time and a place for the reflective growing process but too much time breeds stagnancy.

If you have found yourself stuck for extended periods of time, this card calls you to clear the blockage and get moving.

About the Image on the Card
A pineapple hanging in a fruit stand in Honduras.

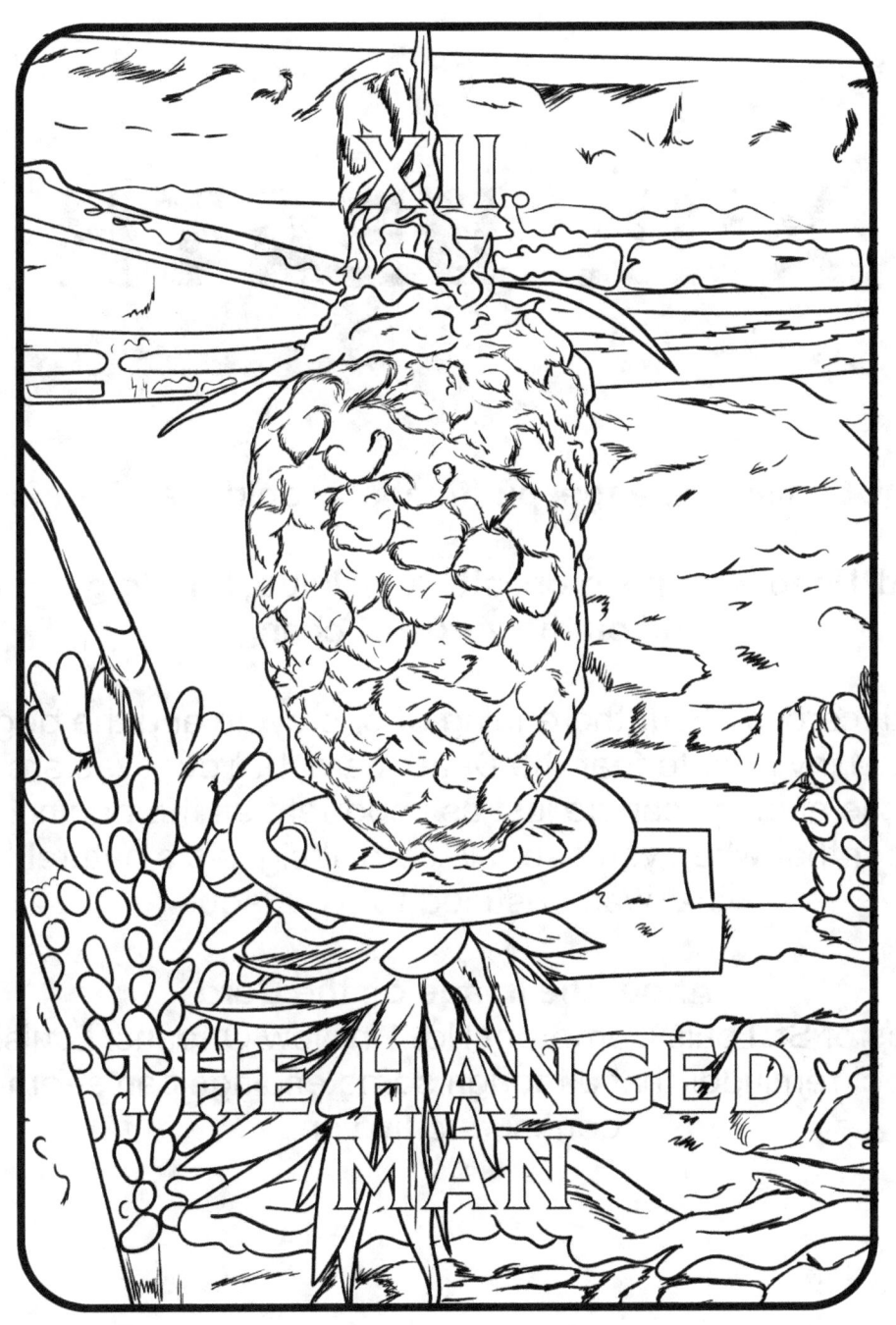

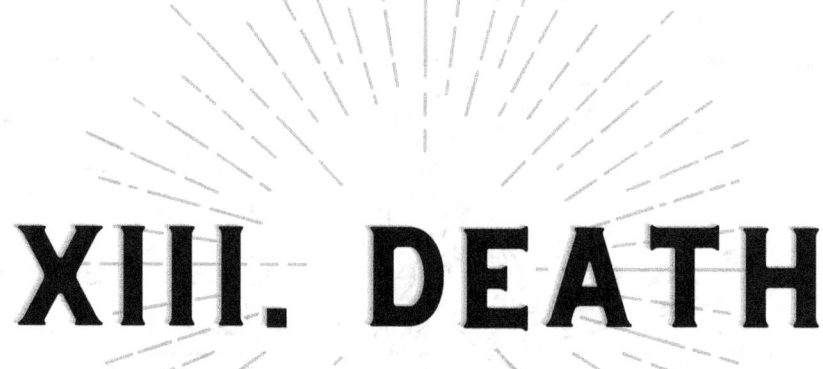

XIII. DEATH

Upright: Endings, change, purification, rebirth, and transitions.

Reversed: Unable to move on, stuck in limbo, letting go of the past, and on the verge of change.

The Death card is about the ending of one cycle and the beginning of another. Many people fear the Death card, but our lives are cyclical and the endings can be just as important as the beginnings. Remember that when you see this card, it signals a natural transition that was destined for your soul.

About the Image on the Card
The tombs of St. Louis Cemetery No. 1 in New Orleans, Louisiana, was the perfect reminder that although some endings can seem final, we continue to live on.

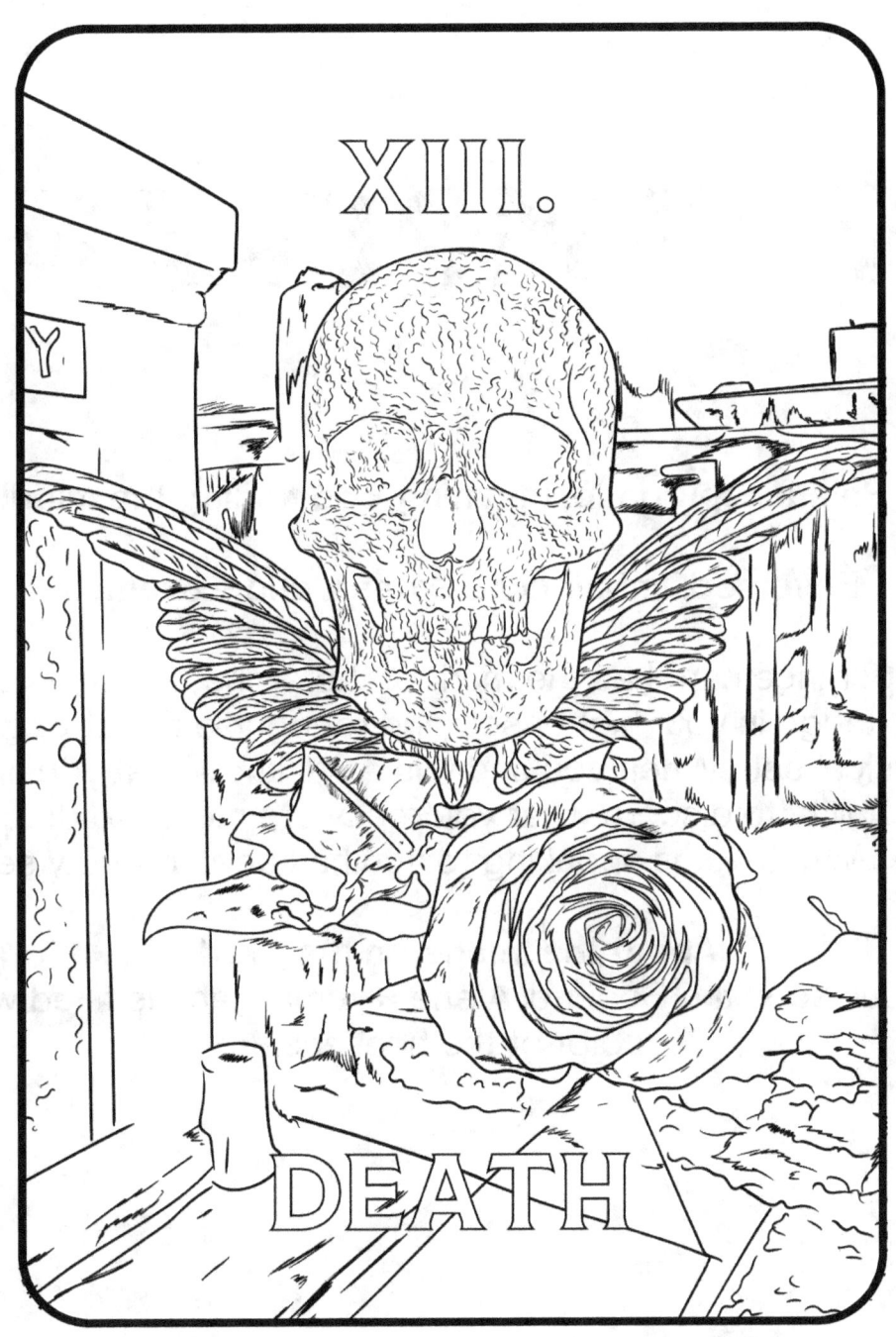

XIV. TEMPERANCE

Upright: Balance, purpose, meaning, and finding the middle road.

Reversed: Imbalance, excess, and extremes.

The Temperance card has the mark of the divine, which helps you to find knowledge in your higher self and recognize the strength within your physical self. When you find this card, know that you are gifted with the ability to discern what you really are meant to do on a soul level. Whatever is speaking to you has been divinely sent.

About the Image on the Card
As the sun sets, the Coeur d' Alene River in Idaho is filled with the color of the heavens.

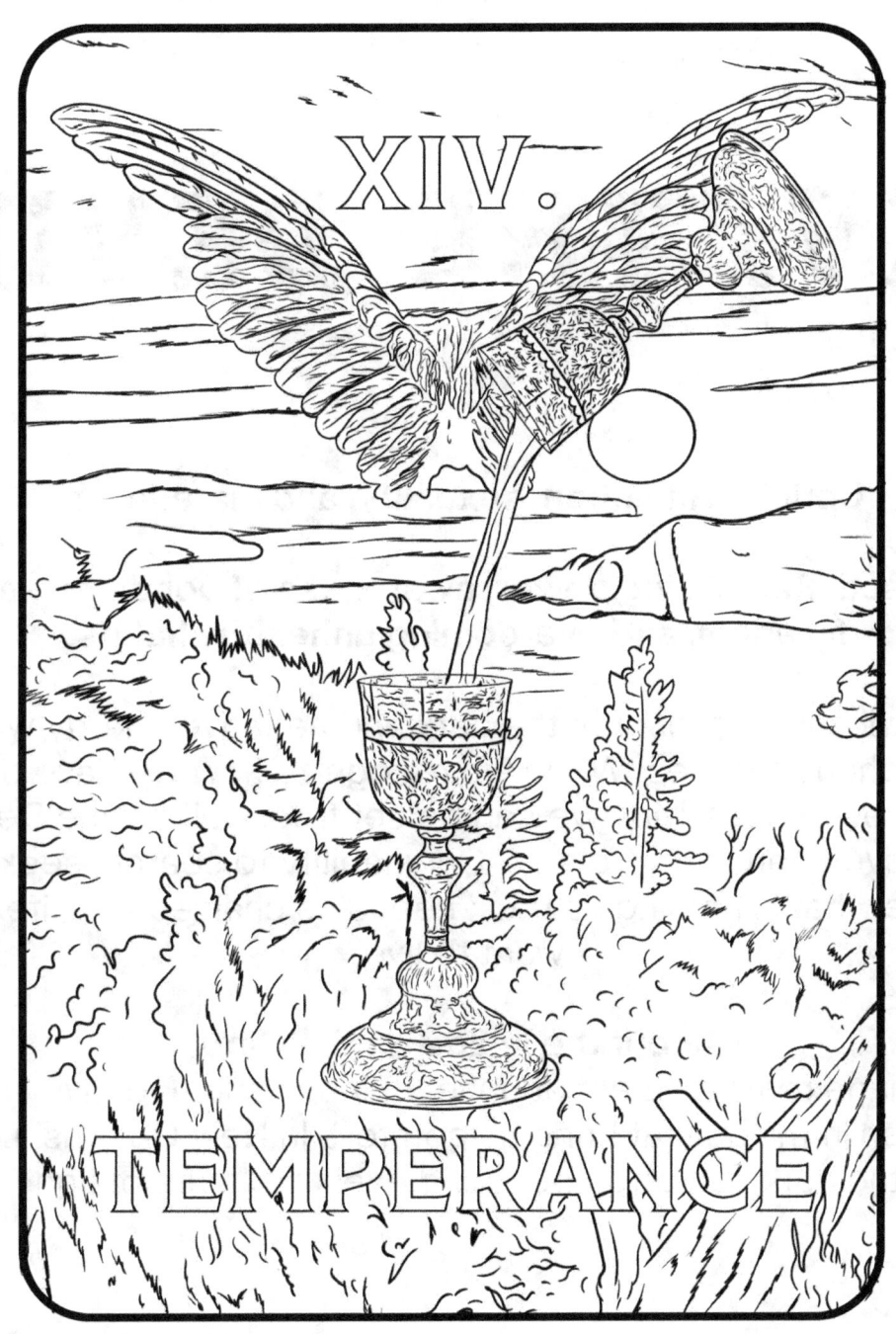

XV. THE DEVIL

Upright: Addiction, sexuality, and materialism

Reversed: Reclaiming power, awareness of bondage, seeking freedom, and overcoming unhealthy habits.

The Devil card represents the dark and negative energy we carry throughout our lives. When we recognize how we have bound ourselves to negativity, we can be set free. Neither the Devil nor negative energy controls us. Our inability to search, seek, and recognize what is holding us back keeps us chained to a life we don't want to live.

About the Image on the Card

This image reminds me that unhealthiness and negativity can be found even in things that bring us comfort. In New Orleans, Louisiana, the dark can often be found even in places of light.

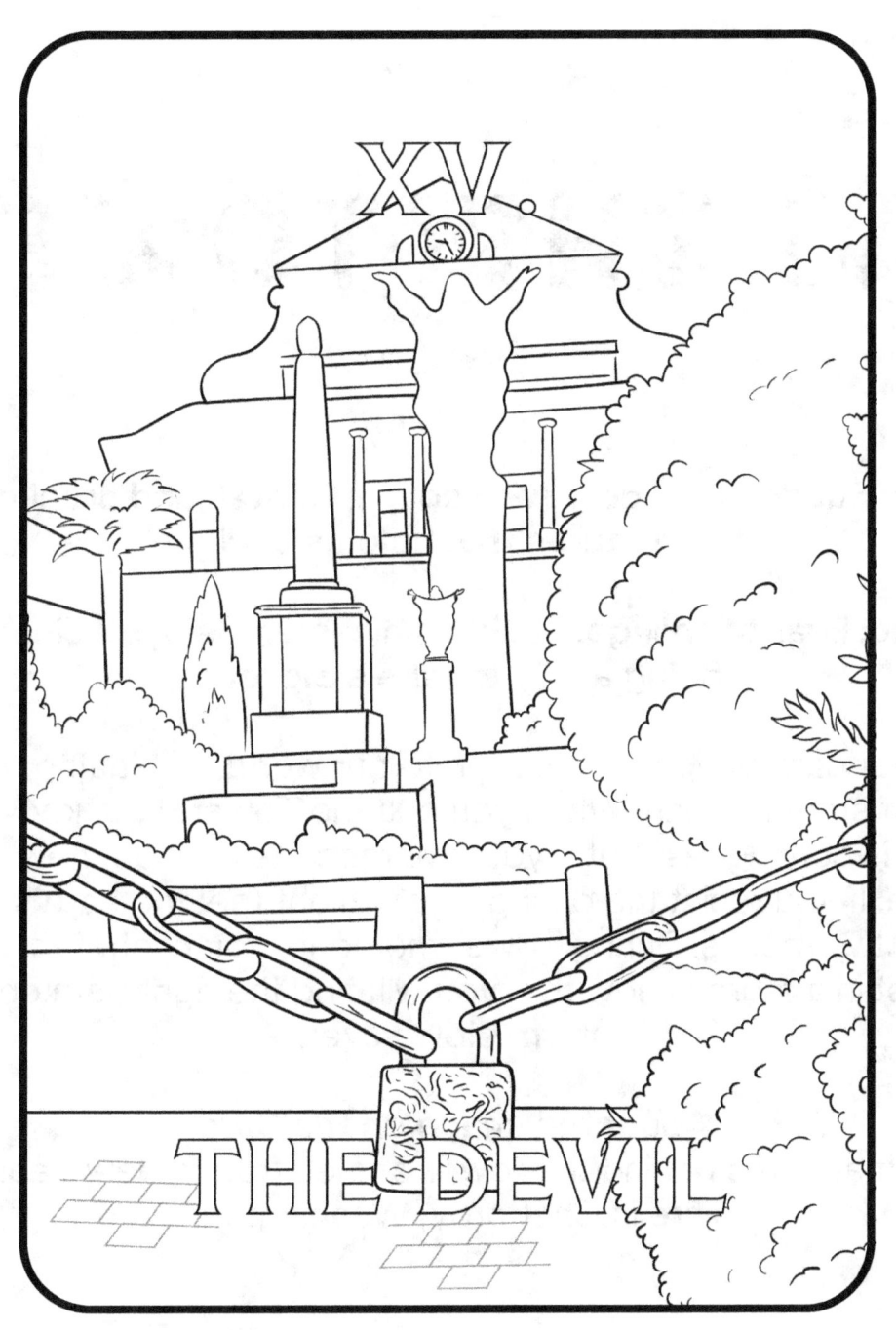

XVI. THE TOWER

Upright: Sudden change, revelation, upheaval, and breakdown of structures that hold us back.

Reversed: Fear of change, avoiding disaster, delayed disaster, and being afraid to take a big leap.

The Tower card brings destruction to our world, but it also brings the gift of starting fresh. When you pull the Tower card, know that change is coming fast but if you embrace the change, new gifts will arrive. If you resist the change, you might feel the card's more destructive means. During Tower moments you might feel like you are lost in a storm; know that you will find the right path once the storm blows over.

About the Image on the Card
The fire that burns behind the tower comes from a New Year's bomb fire in Chattaroy, Washington.

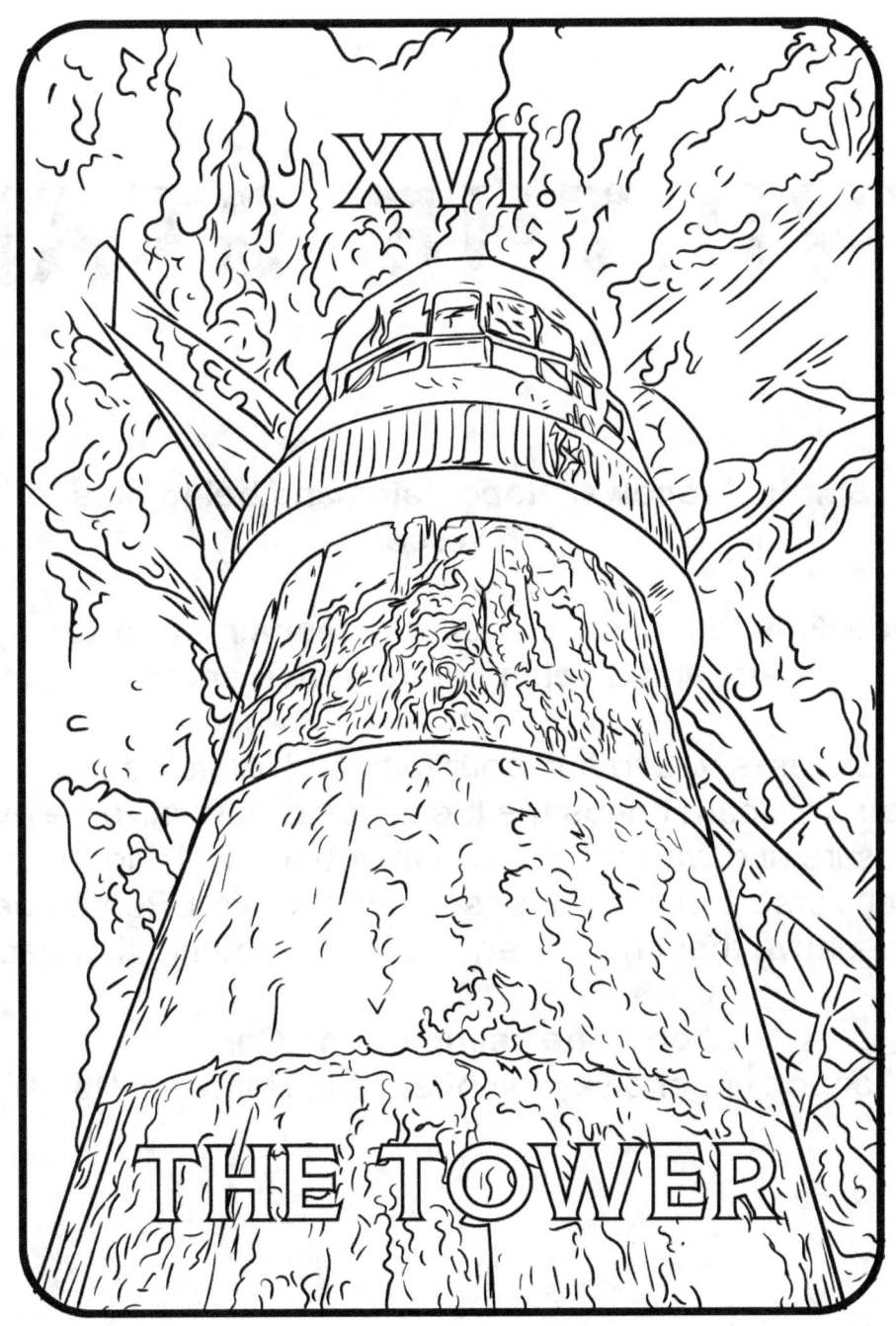

XVII. THE STAR

Upright: Spiritual renewal, hope, faith, and being blessed by the universe.

Reversed: Faithlessness, insecurity, despair, distorted spiritual path, and dwelling on negative energy.

The Star card asks you to find your faith and let its positive and warm light fill you. This card brings the blessings of the universe even when you are unsure and worried. Know that you are walking the path in life that the universe and your inner self want for you. Remember not to dwell on negative thoughts or regrets for something that has passed.

About the Image on the Card
A lagoon under a sky full of stars in Honolulu, Hawaii.

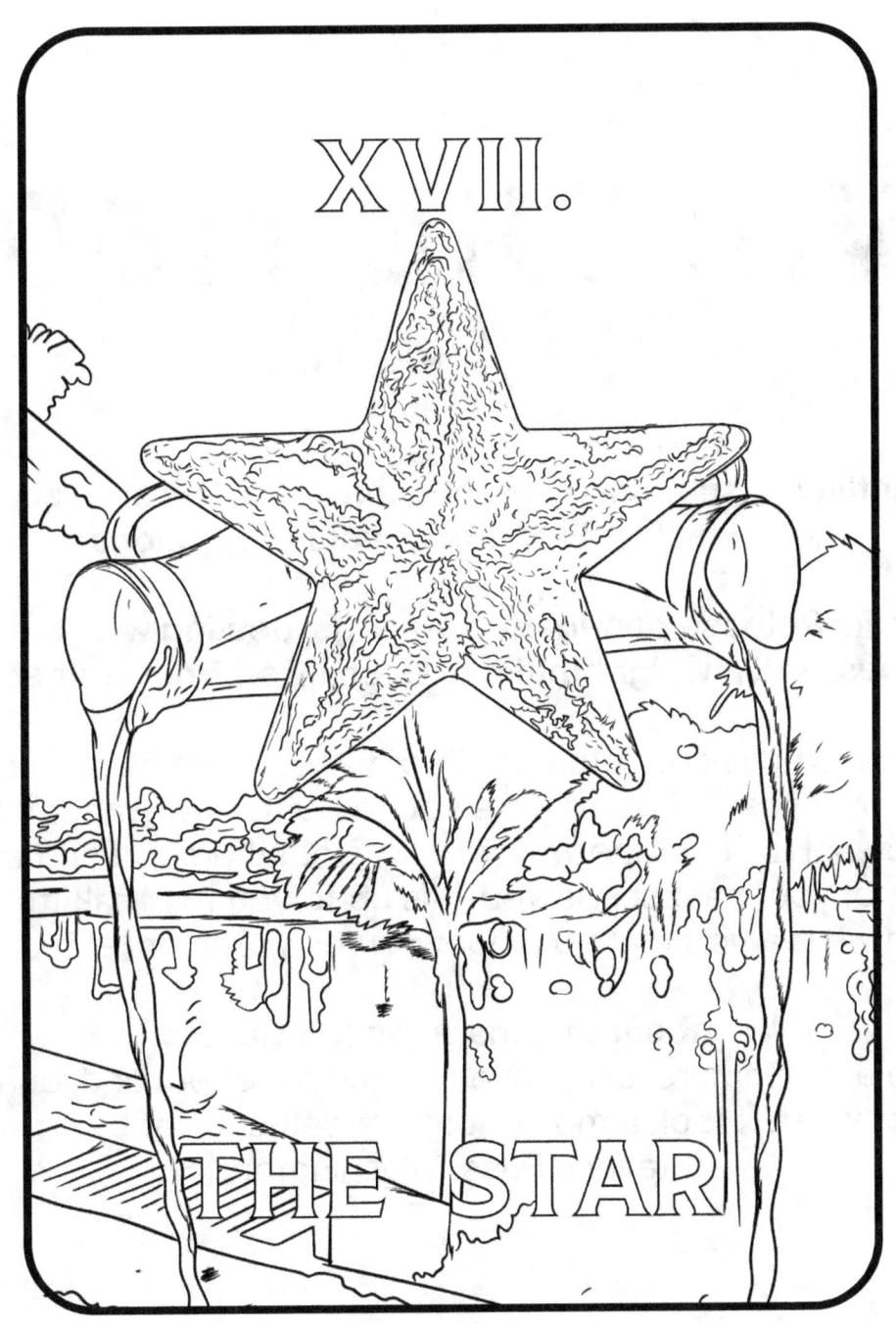

XVIII. THE MOON

Upright: Intuition, subconscious, illusions, shadow self, and a call to be consciously aware of your projections.

Reversed: Release of negative feelings, dealing with emotional issues, and a weight that has been lifted from your soul.

The Moon card is about the depth of the subconscious and how it affects our lives. This card asks you to do the work and to look at why you act or react the way you do. Both the good and the bad moments of your past shape you. It is up to you to break free of what you have learned that no longer serves you in order to grow.

About the Image on the Card
A quiet place in nature is my favorite time to reflect and journal. This is a spot where I took a moment for myself and sat by a river near Stevens Pass, Washington.

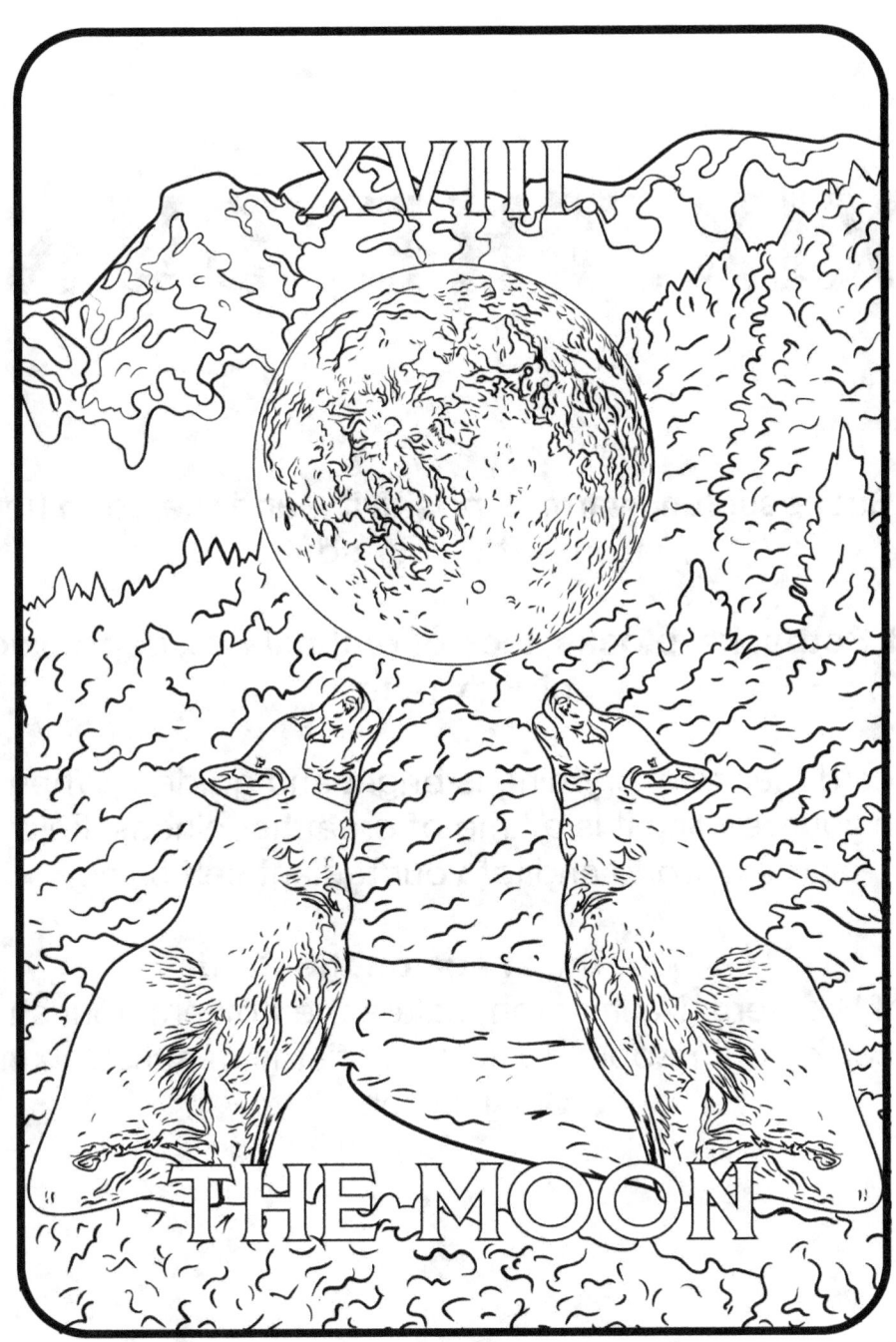

XIX. THE SUN

Upright: Success, fun, warmth, positivity, and the deep happiness from within our soul.

Reversed: Setbacks, blocks, lack of enthusiasm, depression, and a cloudy path.

The Sun card means everything is bright and golden. When you see this card in your reading it is a time of great happiness. Enjoy yourself and the world and let your radiant self shine.

About the Image on the Card
The rain of Western Washington makes the flowers flourish so when the sun comes out people flock to the fields of sunshine in Duvall, Washington.

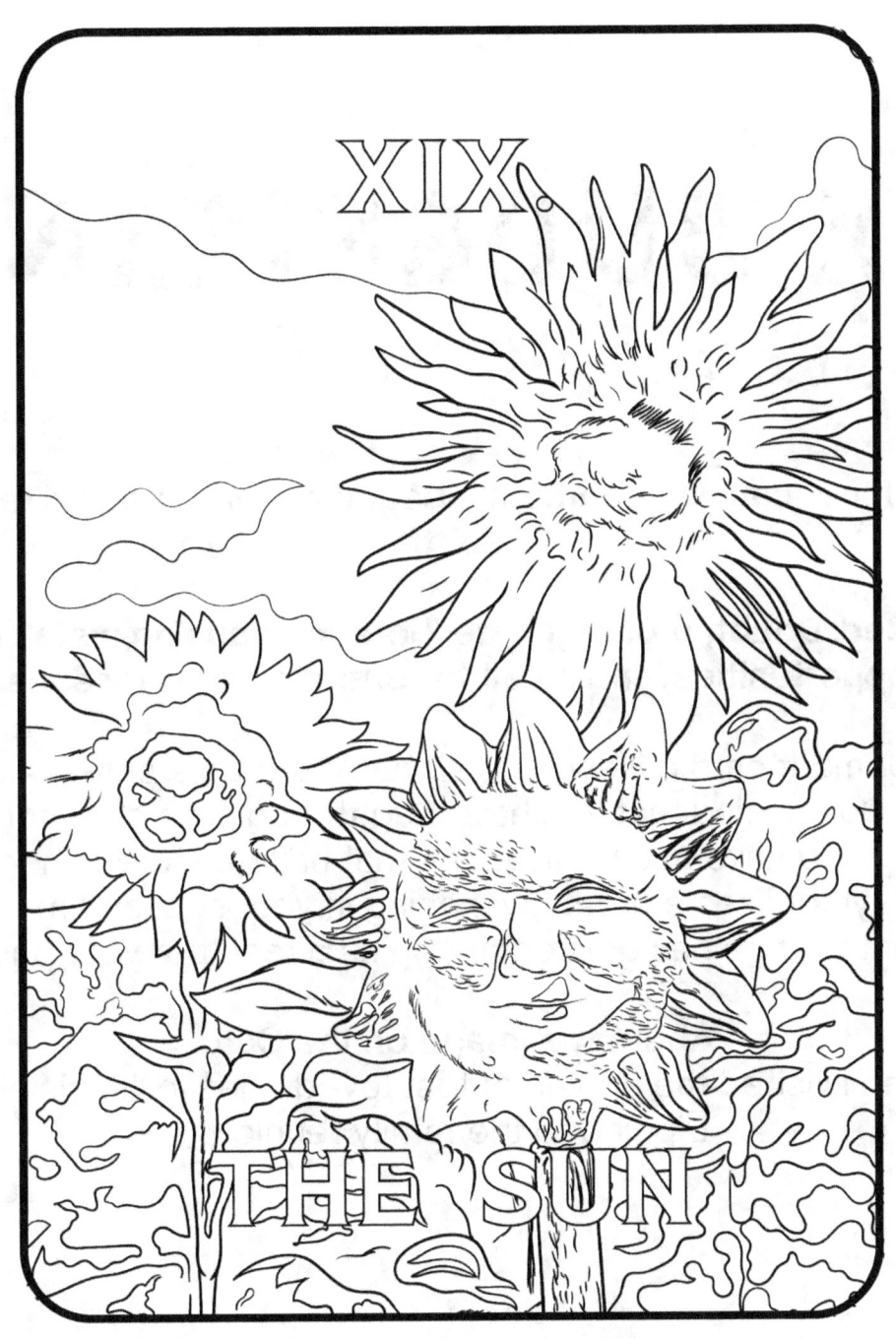

XX. JUDGEMENT

Upright: Inner calling, judgment, absolution, and the end leading to rebirth.

Reversed: Doubt, prolonged deliberation causing a stall in new opportunities, and a call to reflect on past lessons.

The Judgement card calls you to sit back and do a self-evaluation of your life. Do you find that you have dug through the common themes in your life and have had realizations that have enacted change? This card symbolizes a great awakening in your soul and means a significant change has or is occurring as a result of your past work.

About the Image on the Card
From when I visited the graves of lost loved ones in Illinois while road tripping to the family reunion.

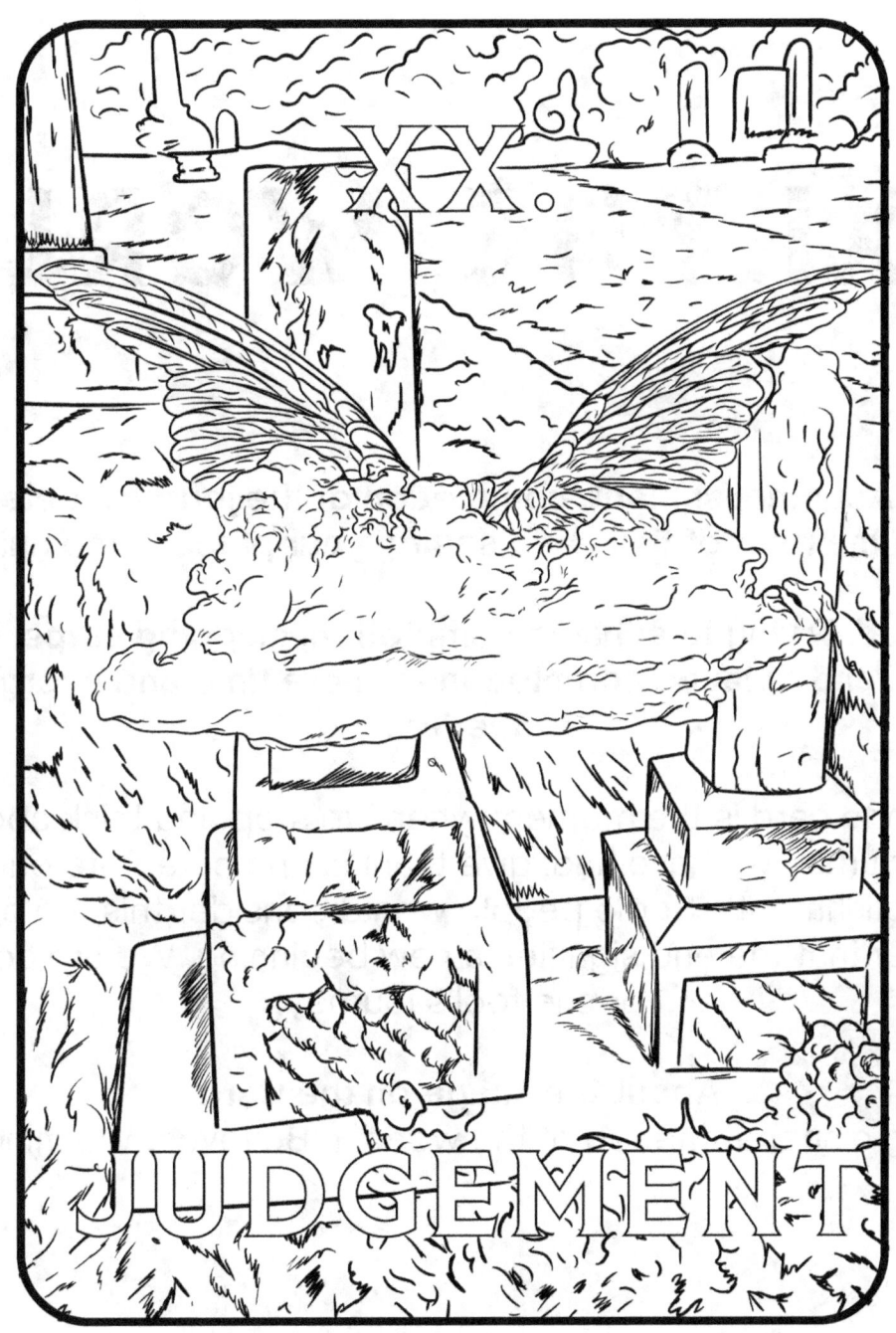

XXI. THE WORLD

Upright: Accomplishment, completion of the journey, celebration; you are the ruler of time, and seeing your place in the universe.

Reversed: Trying to achieve completion, skipping steps, loss of focus, and delayed completion as more time and energy are needed.

The World card is the moment when we stop and think about the journey we have had, give thanks, and celebrate our accomplishments. Some people would consider this the end, but remember that the end signifies a new beginning. We are constantly on the fool's journey.

About the Image on the Card
Having dinner at the top of the world in Bellevue, Washington.

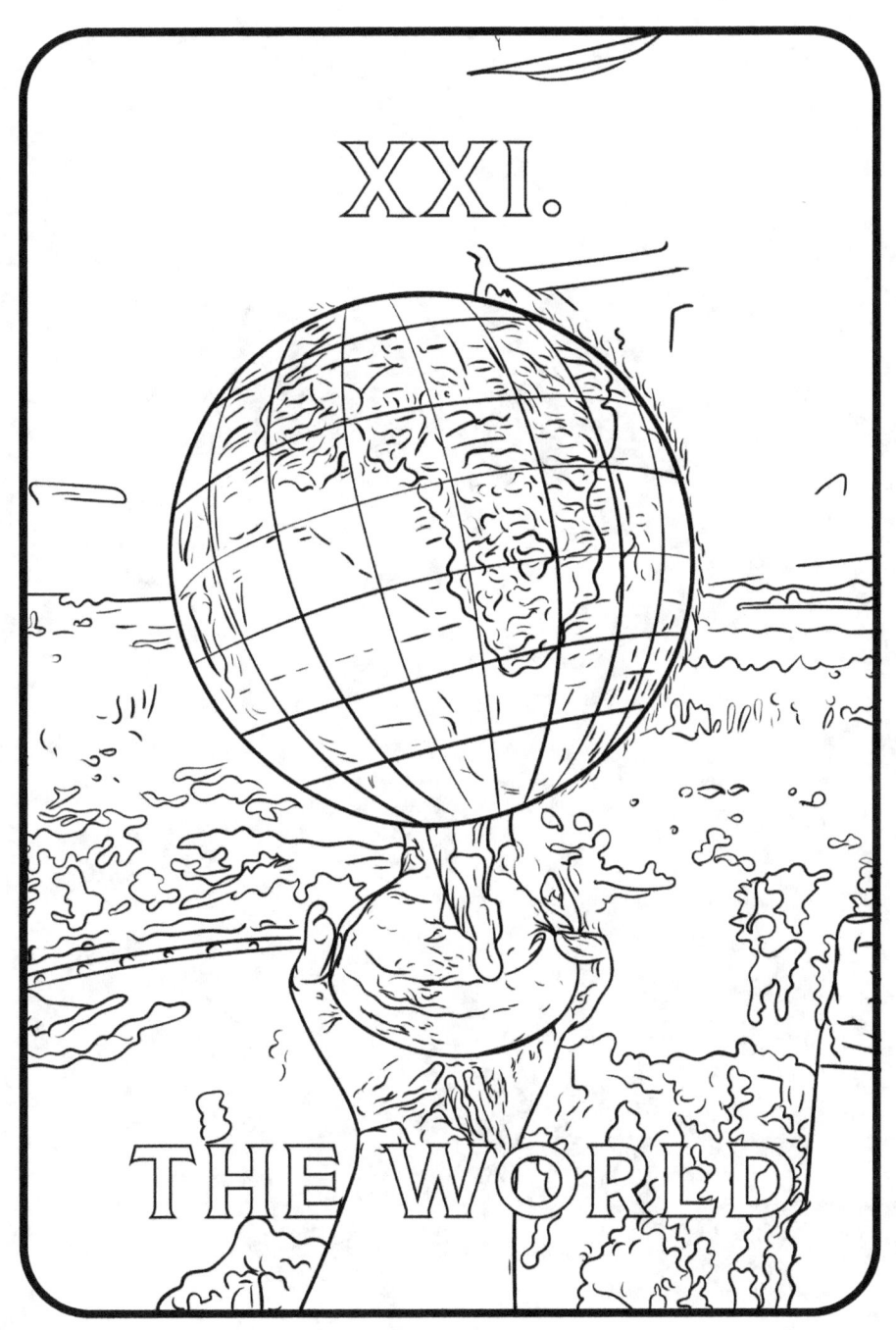

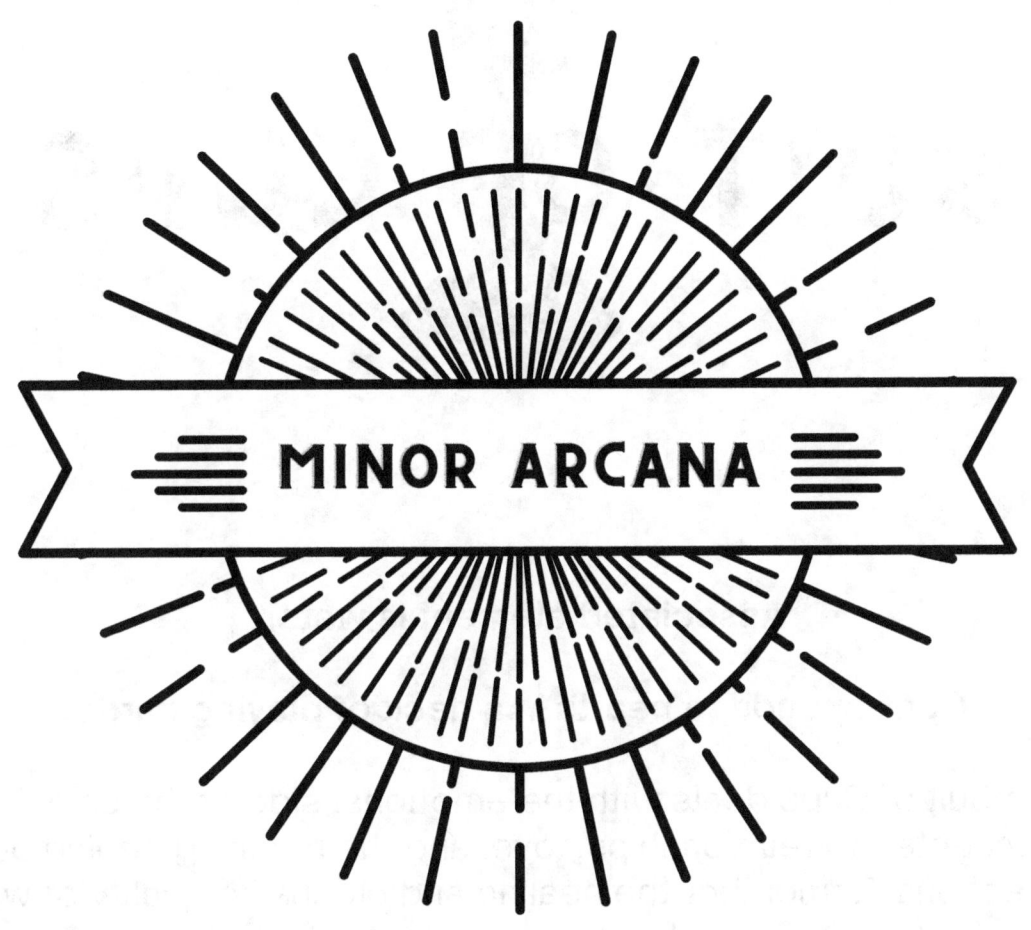

MINOR ARCANA

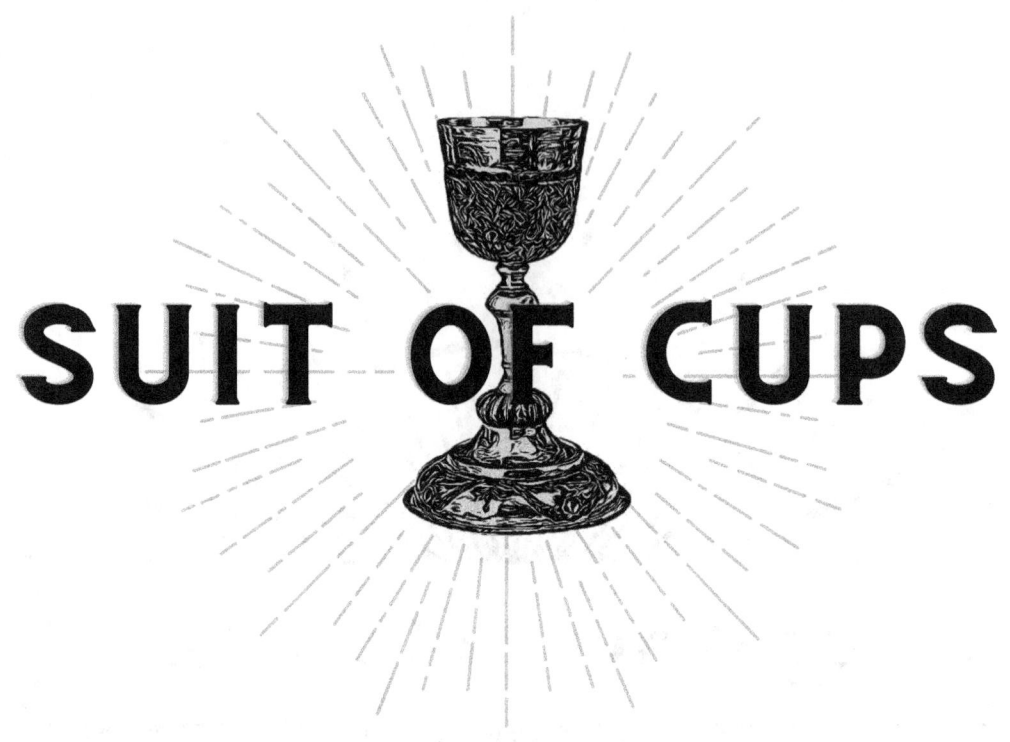

SUIT OF CUPS

Associated element is water.

Corresponds to hearts in a deck of playing cards.

The Suit of Cups deals with the emotional side of the soul. It is connected to relationships, love, and the meaning behind our connections. Remember the healing and cleansing quality of water. Let it rinse over your soul.

Questions to consider with a Suit of Cups card:
What am I feeling? Look at the story of the card's meaning and how your emotions and feelings are connected to it.

What emotions become connected as a result of this card being pulled, and what do they mean?

What thoughts surface as you read the meaning of the card?

SUIT OF CUPS QUICK GUIDE

Ace of Cups
Upright: Overwhelming emotion, love, and creativity.

Reversed: Missed opportunities, blocked creativity, and emotional issues or loss.

About the Wandering Traveler card: Couples walking through the waves at Sunset Beach Park in Honolulu, Hawaii.

Two of Cups
Upright: Love, unity, and connection.

Reversed: Trust issues, imbalance, and tension.

About the Wandering Traveler card: Birthday dinner at Beverly's Restaurant in Couer d'Alene, Idaho, complete with cotton candy dessert.

Three of Cups
Upright: Community, friendship, and happiness.

Reversed: Gossip, overindulgence, and feeling distanced.

About the Wandering Traveler card: Three of the tastiest Mint Juleps you can get at the Oak Alley Plantation in Vacherie, Louisiana.

Four of Cups
Upright: Plateau, reevaluation, and contemplation.

Reversed: Bitter, angry, and apathetic.

About the Wandering Traveler card: The beautiful Red Rock hills in Sedona, Arizona.

Five of Cups
Upright: Loss, regret, and bereavement.

Reversed: Moving on, finding peace, and forgiveness.

About the Wandering Traveler card: The tombs at the St. Louis Cemetery No. 1 in New Orleans, Louisiana.

Six of Cups
Upright: Nostalgia, reunion, and happy memories.

Reversed: Living in the past, false memories, and unable to move forward.

About the Wandering Traveler card: A wild country garden in Snohomish, Washington.

SUIT OF CUPS
QUICK GUIDE

Seven of Cups
Upright: Wishful thinking, illusion, and imagination.

Reversed: Distraction, temptation, and lack of purpose.

About the Wandering Traveler card:
Just pick a beach: an unhelpful sign on the island of Roatán in Honduras.

Eight of Cups
Upright: Walking away, abandonment, and escapism.

Reversed: Hopelessness, drifting through life, and avoidance.

About the Wandering Traveler card:
A path into the woods in Monroe, Washington.

Nine of Cups
Upright: Luxurious comfort, satisfaction, and fulfilled.

Reversed: Dissatisfaction, greed, and lack of inner joy.

About the Wandering Traveler card:
A perfect rainbow in Snohomish, Washington.

Ten of Cups
Upright: Marriage, harmony, and dreams coming true.

Reversed: Broken relationship, shattered dreams, and disharmony in the home.

About the Wandering Traveler card:
A beach meant for love in Los Cabos, Mexico.

Page of Cups
Upright: Creative beginnings, dreamer, and synchronicity.

Reversed: Creative block, emotional immaturity, and no foresight.

About the Wandering Traveler card:
A quiet beach on Camano Island, Washington.

Knight of Cups
Upright: Romance, idealist, and following your heart.

Reversed: Disappointment, jealousy, and unrealistic.

About the Wandering Traveler card:
Horseback riding through the sand and the surf at Long Beach, Washington.

SUIT OF CUPS QUICK GUIDE

Queen of Cups
Upright: Intuitive, calm, and compassionate.

Reversed: Codependent, insecurity, and martyrdom.

About the Wandering Traveler card:
The lapping waves on Anastasia Island, Florida.

King of Cups
Upright: Emotional balance, control, and compassion.

Reversed: Manipulation, moodiness, and volatility.

About the Wandering Traveler card:
Sunset sailboat ride in Honolulu, Hawaii.

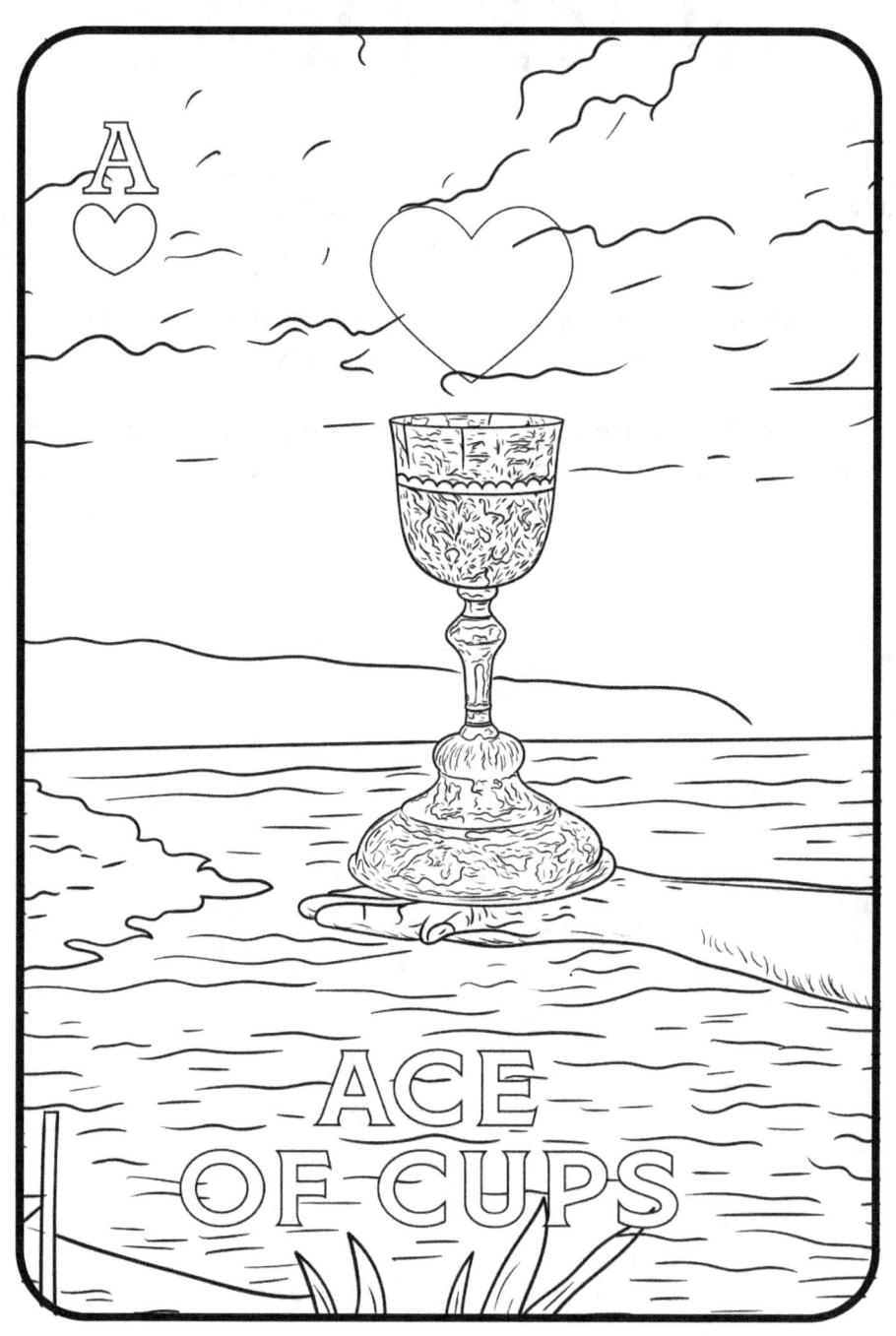

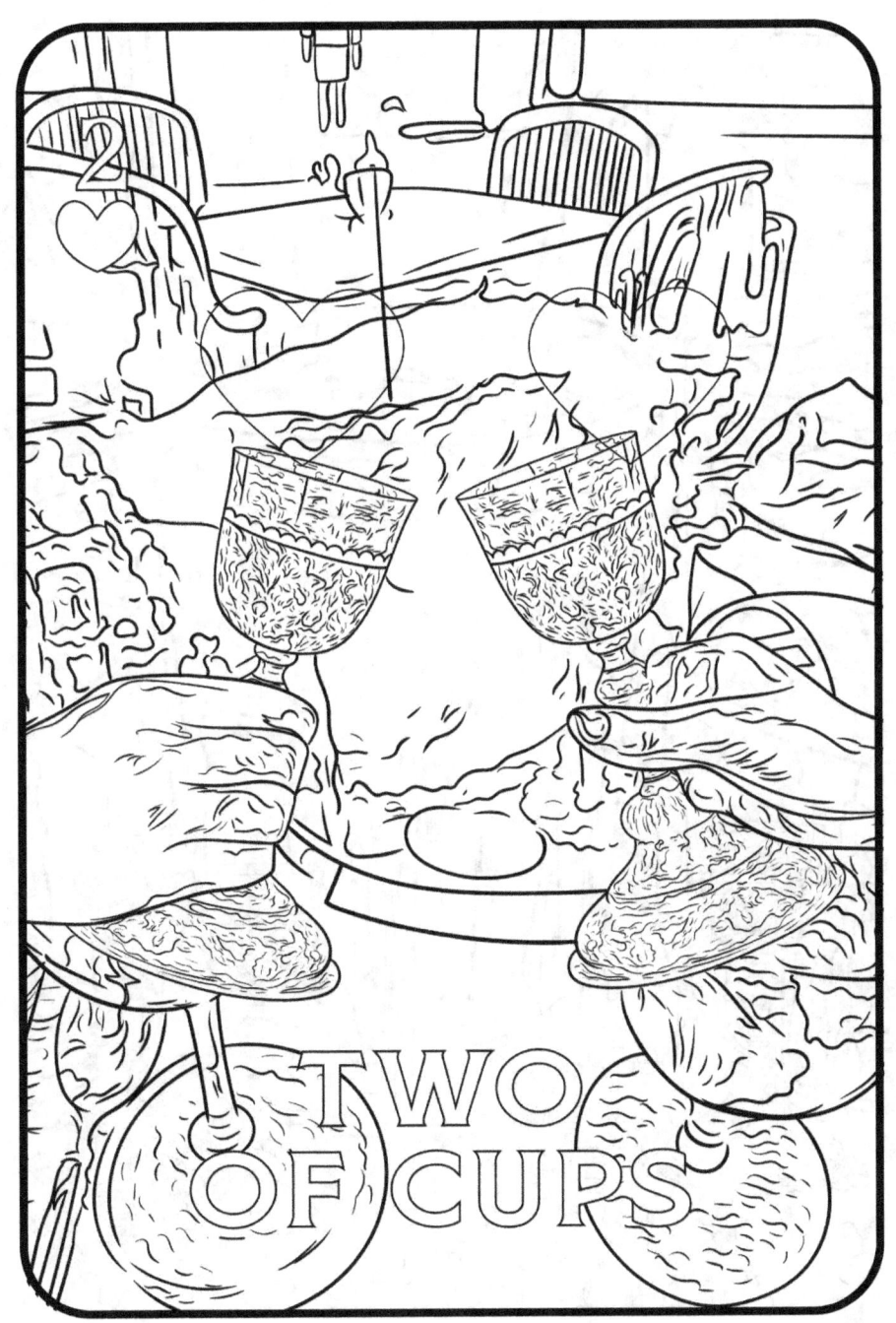

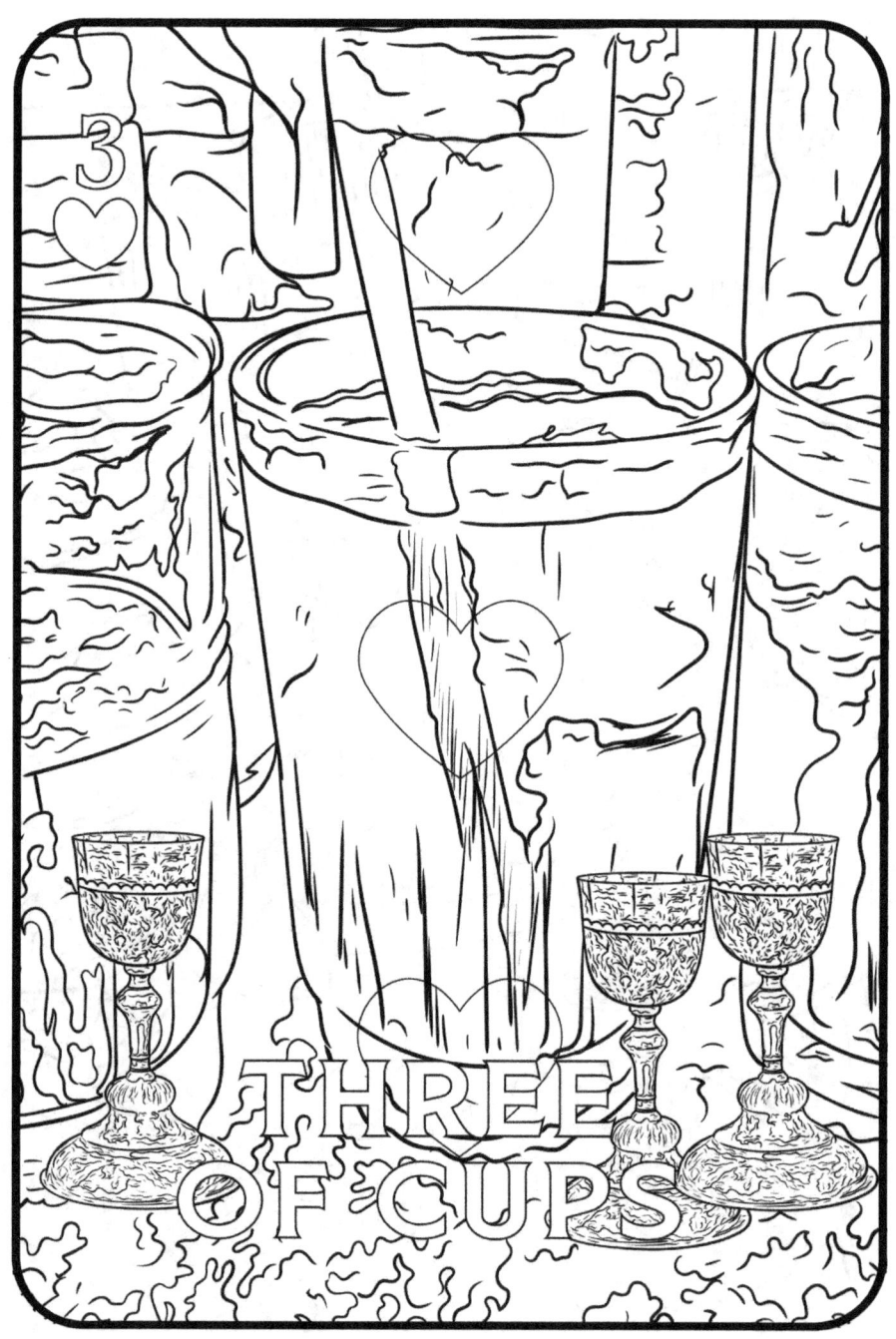

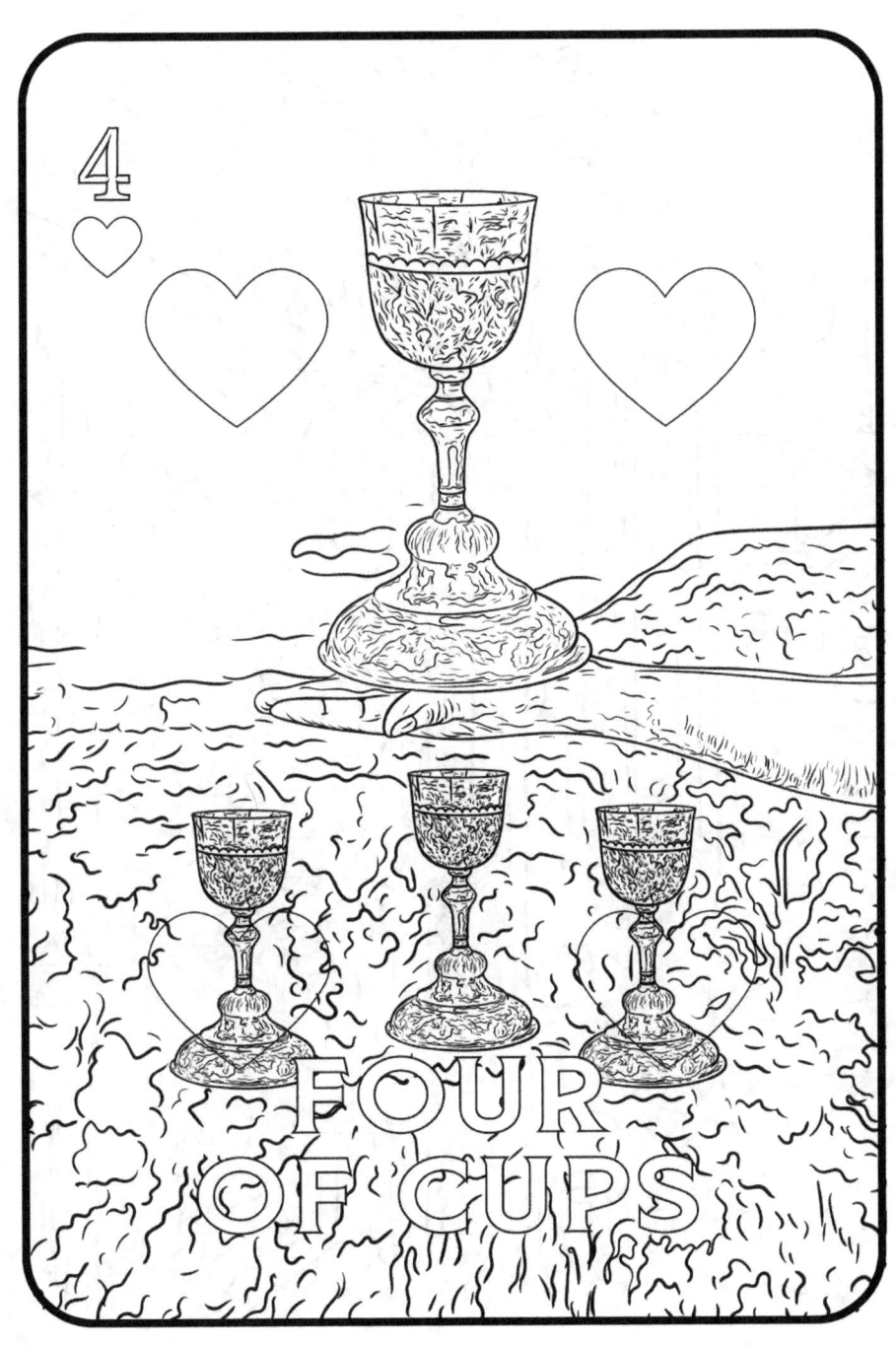

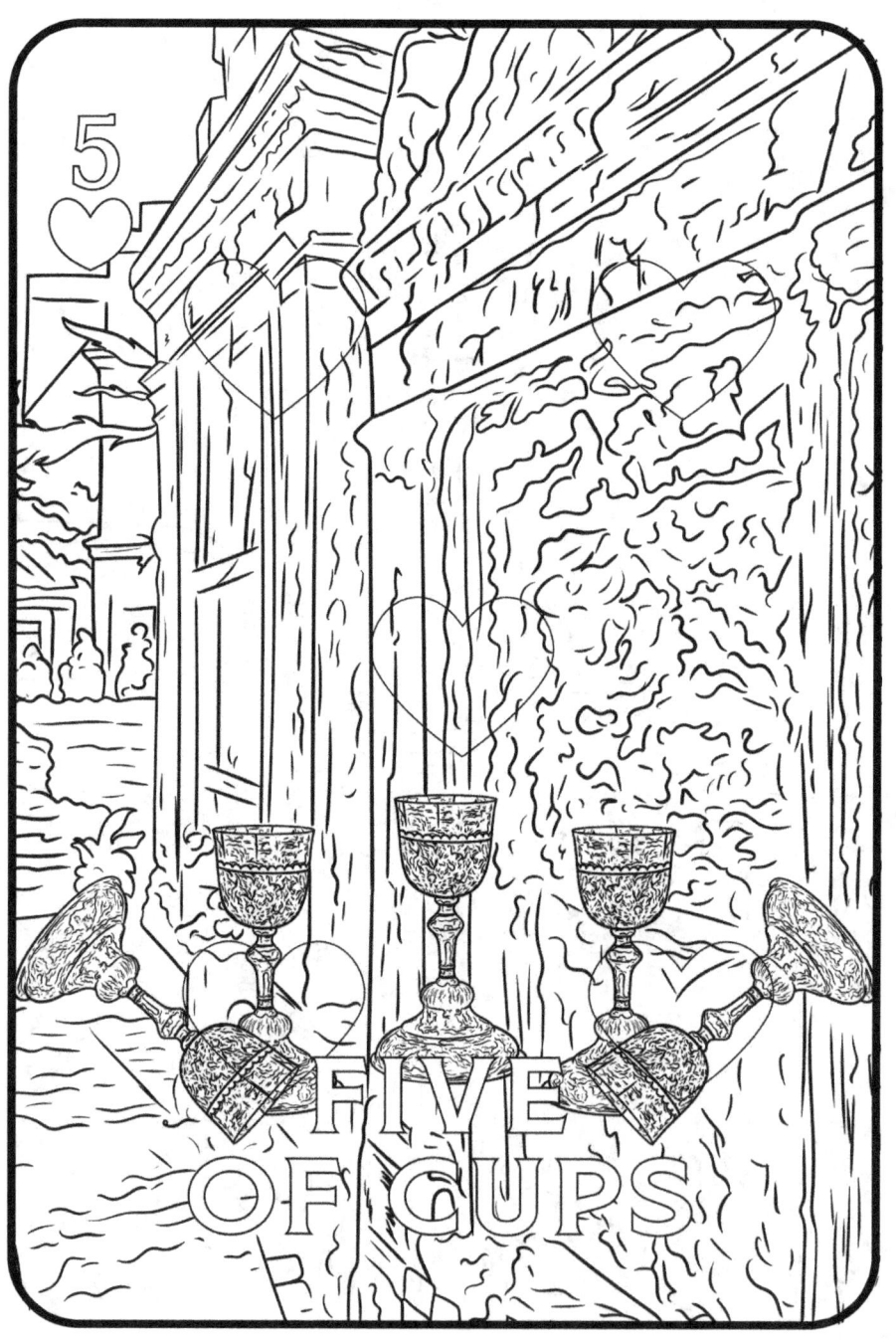

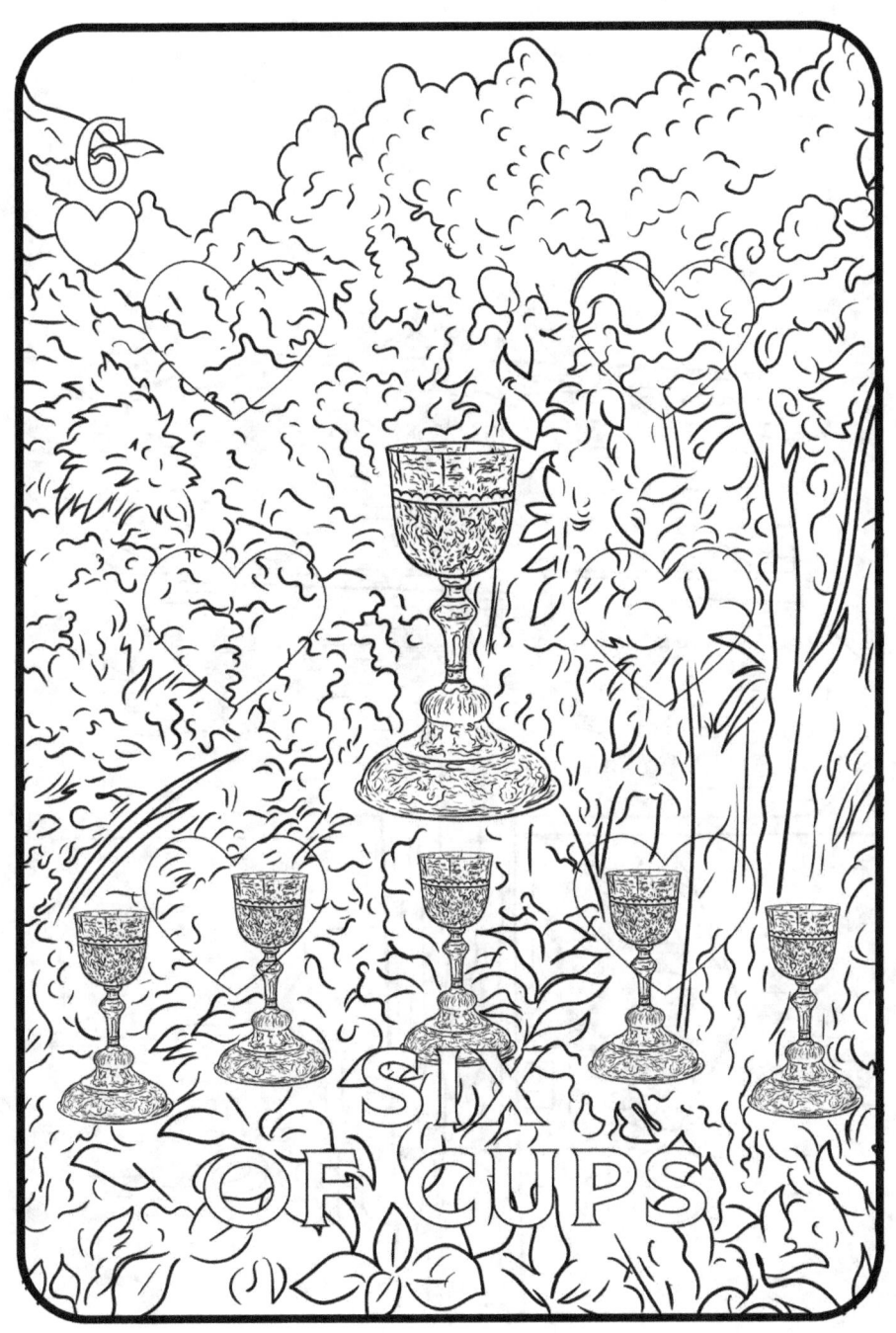

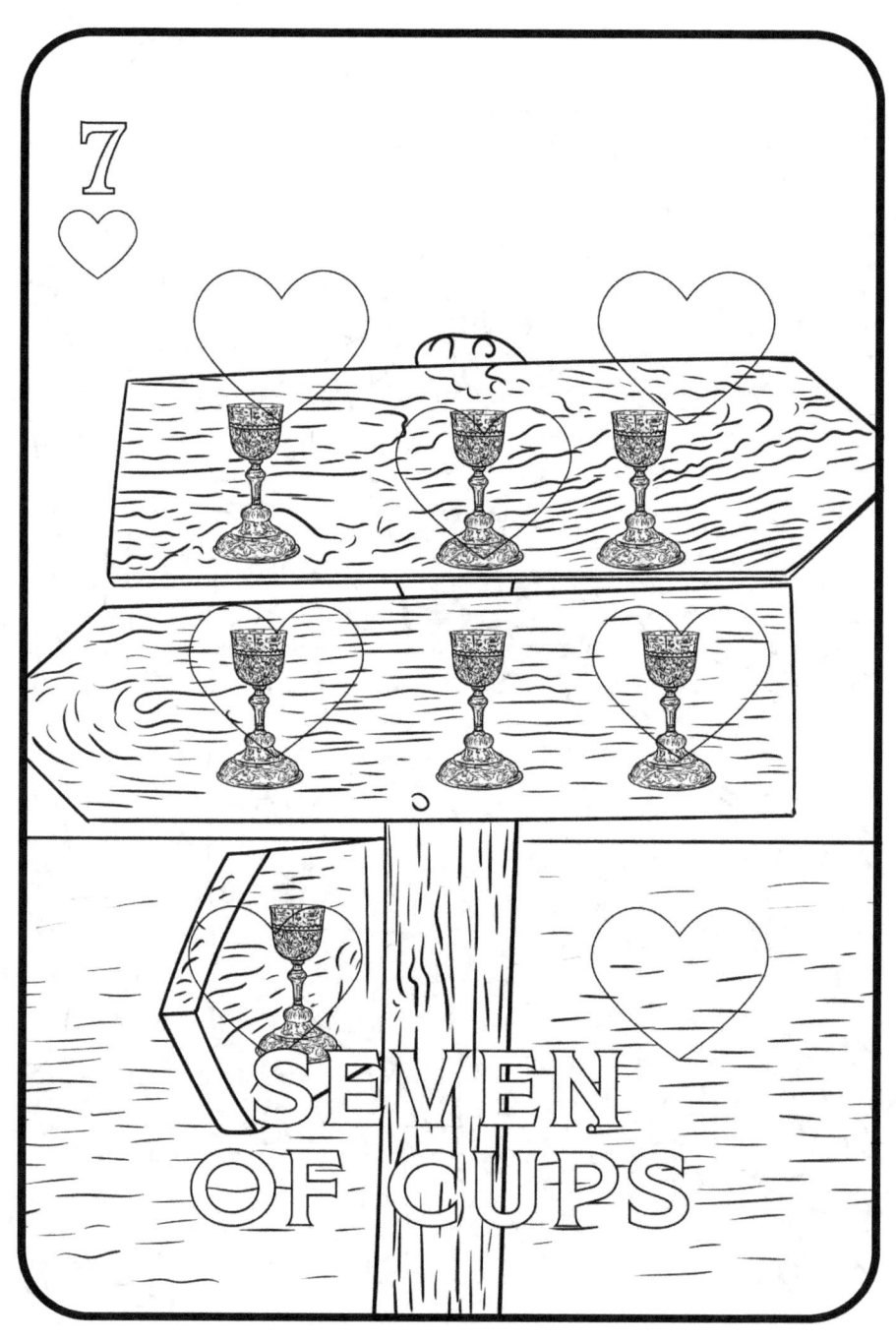

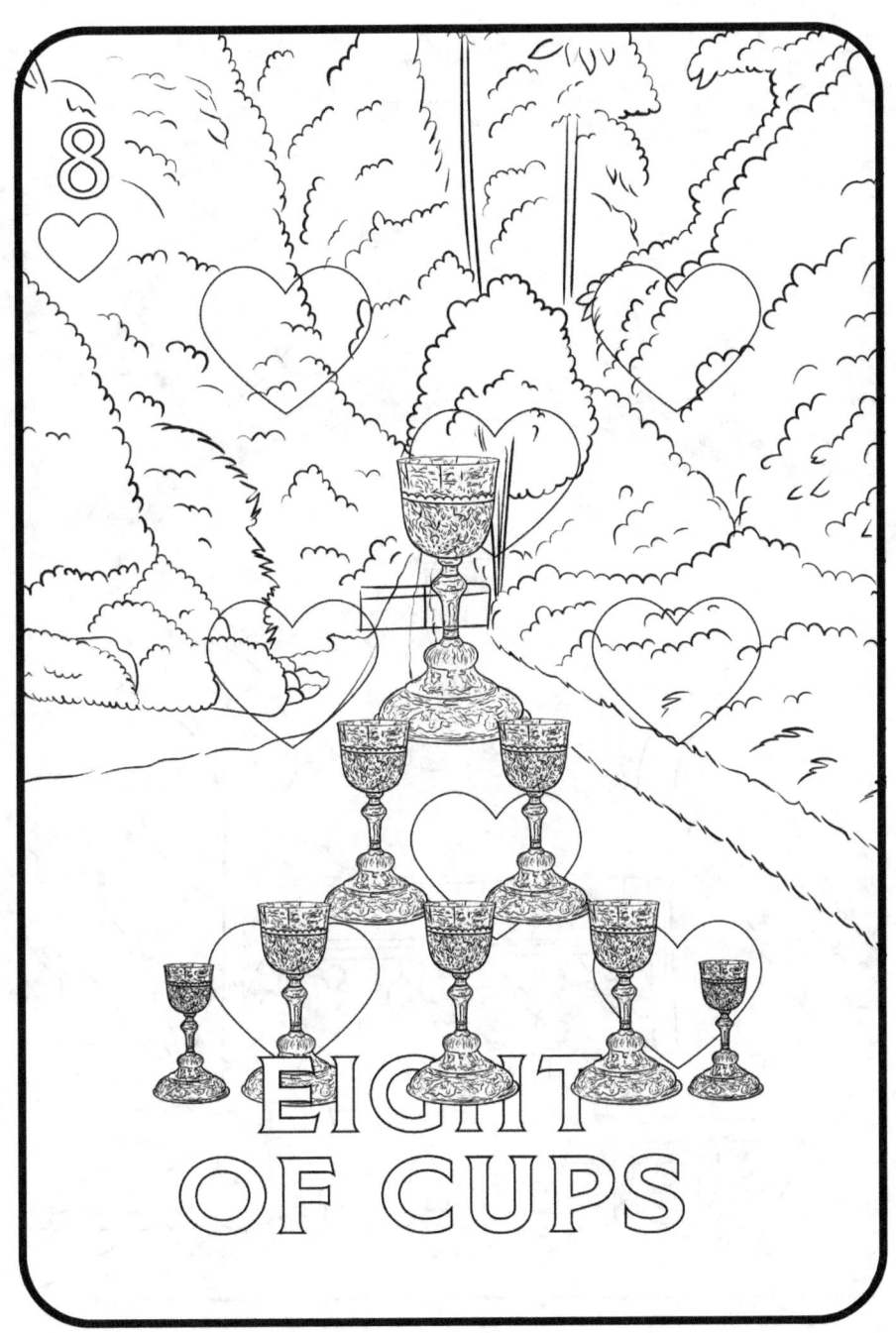

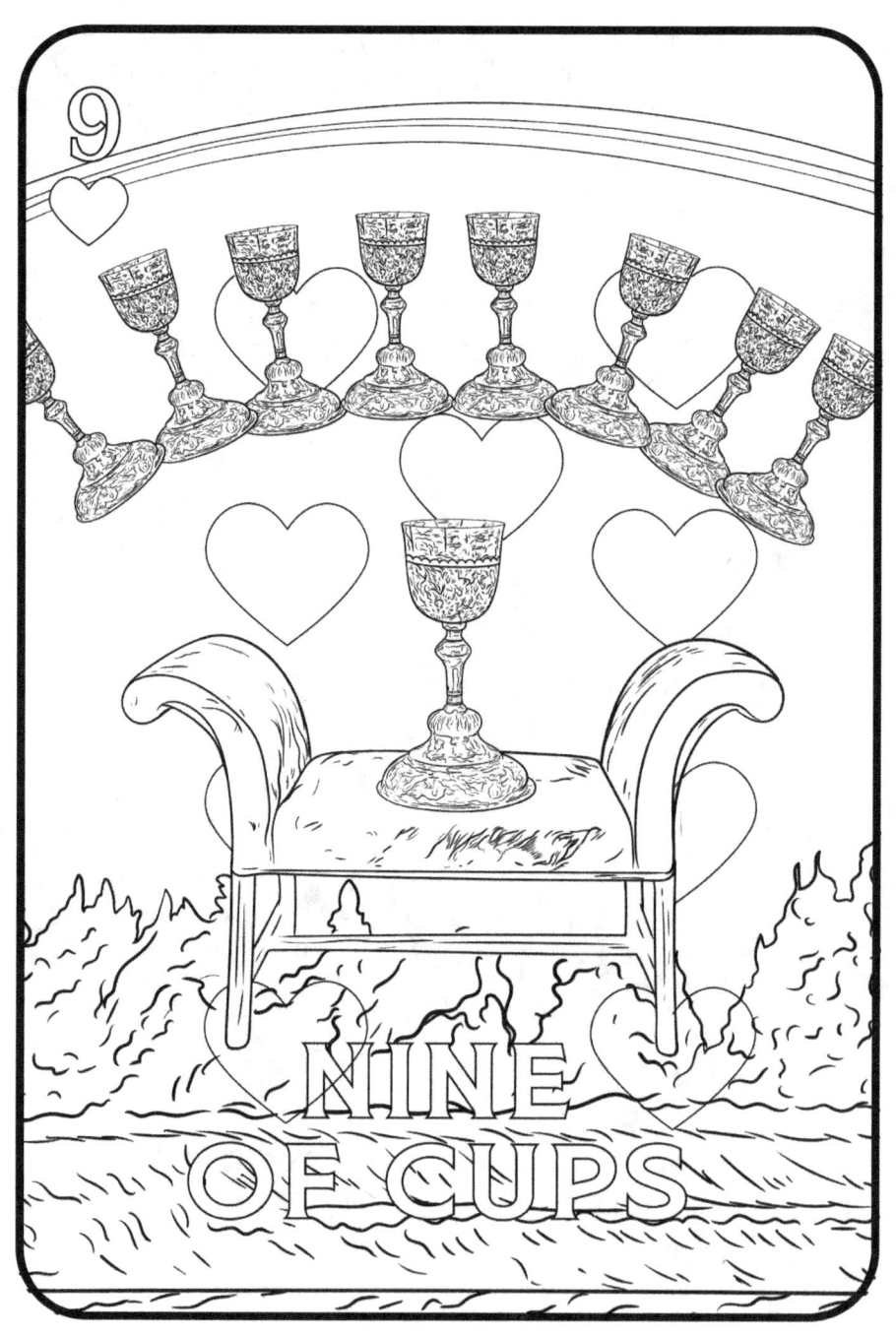

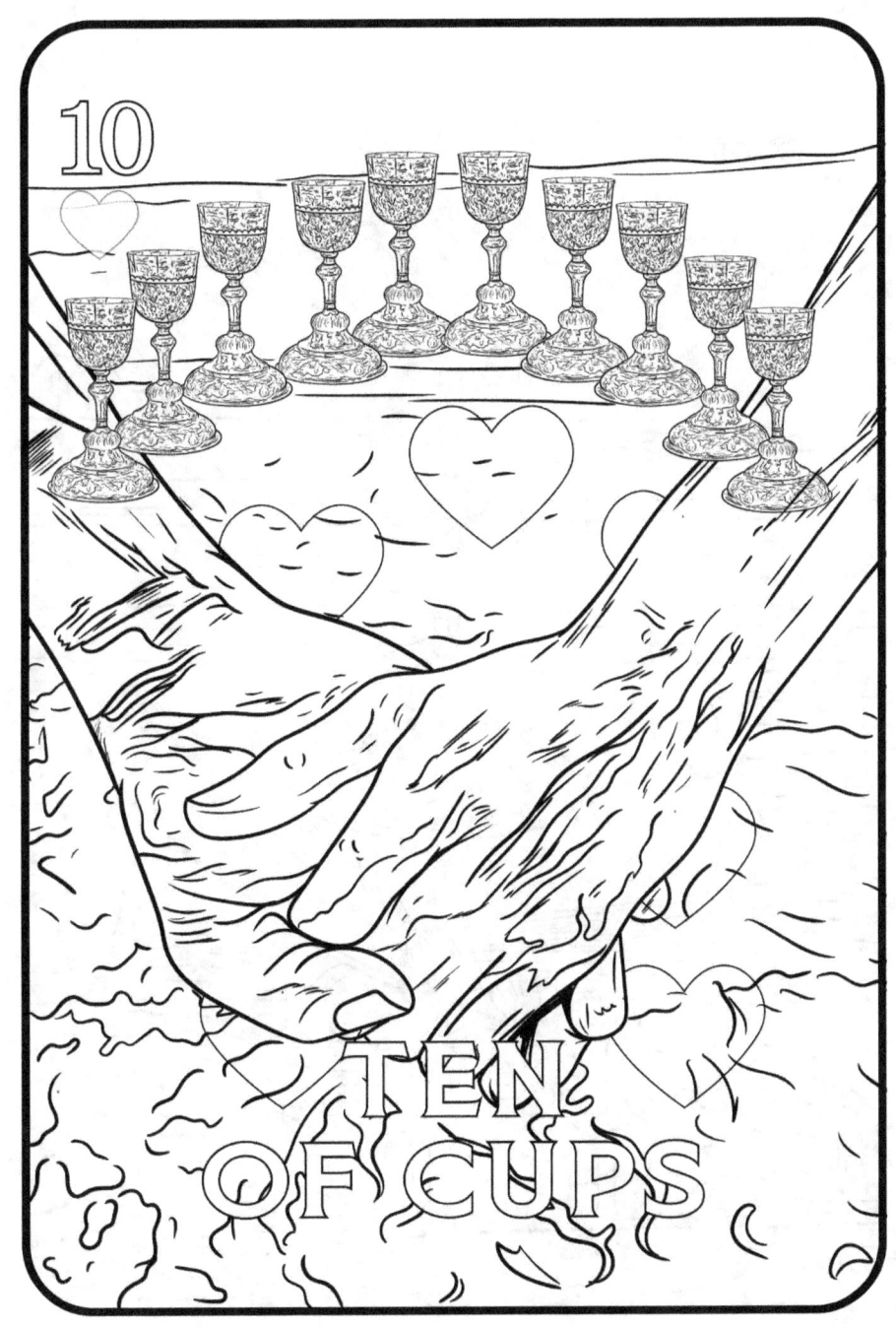

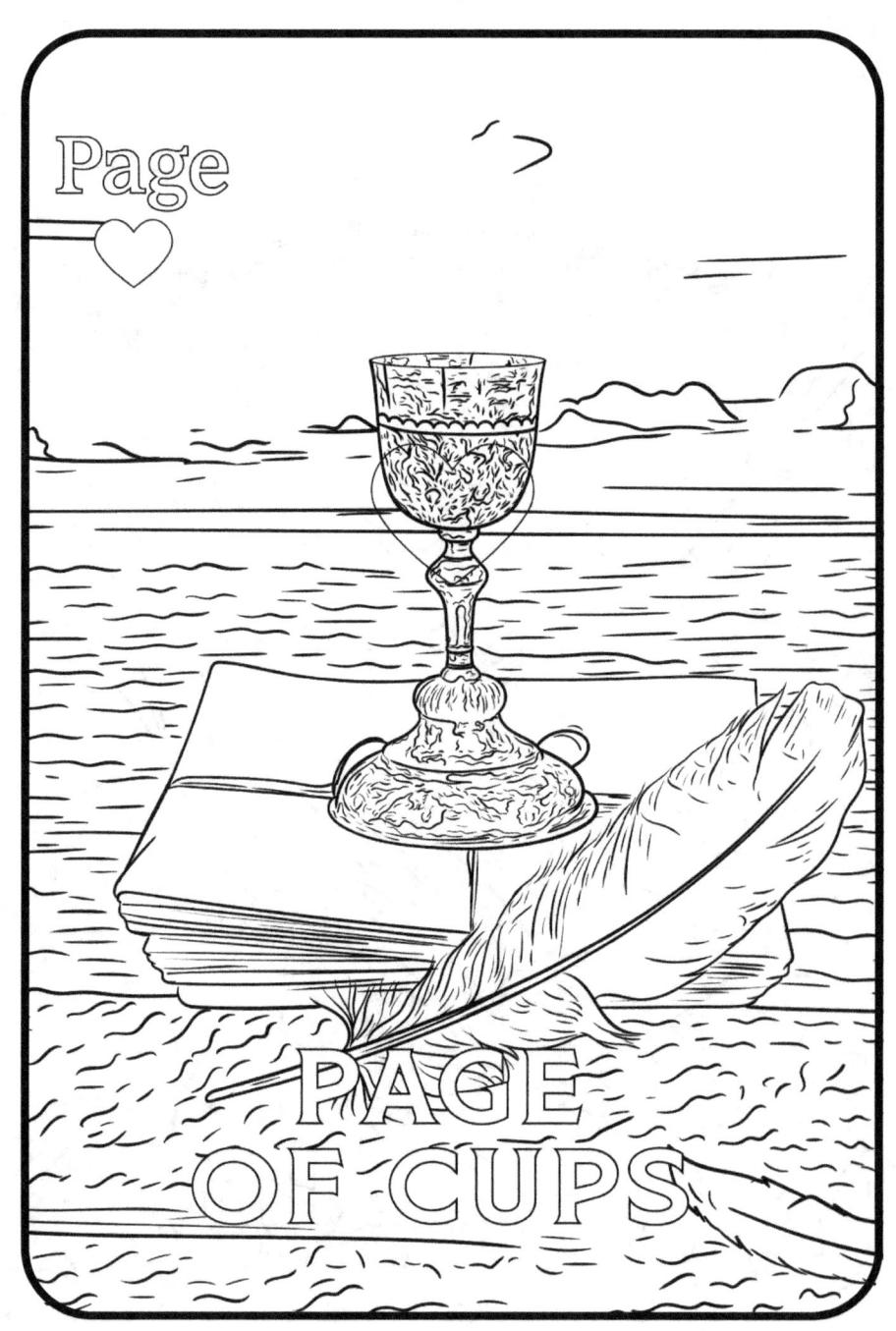

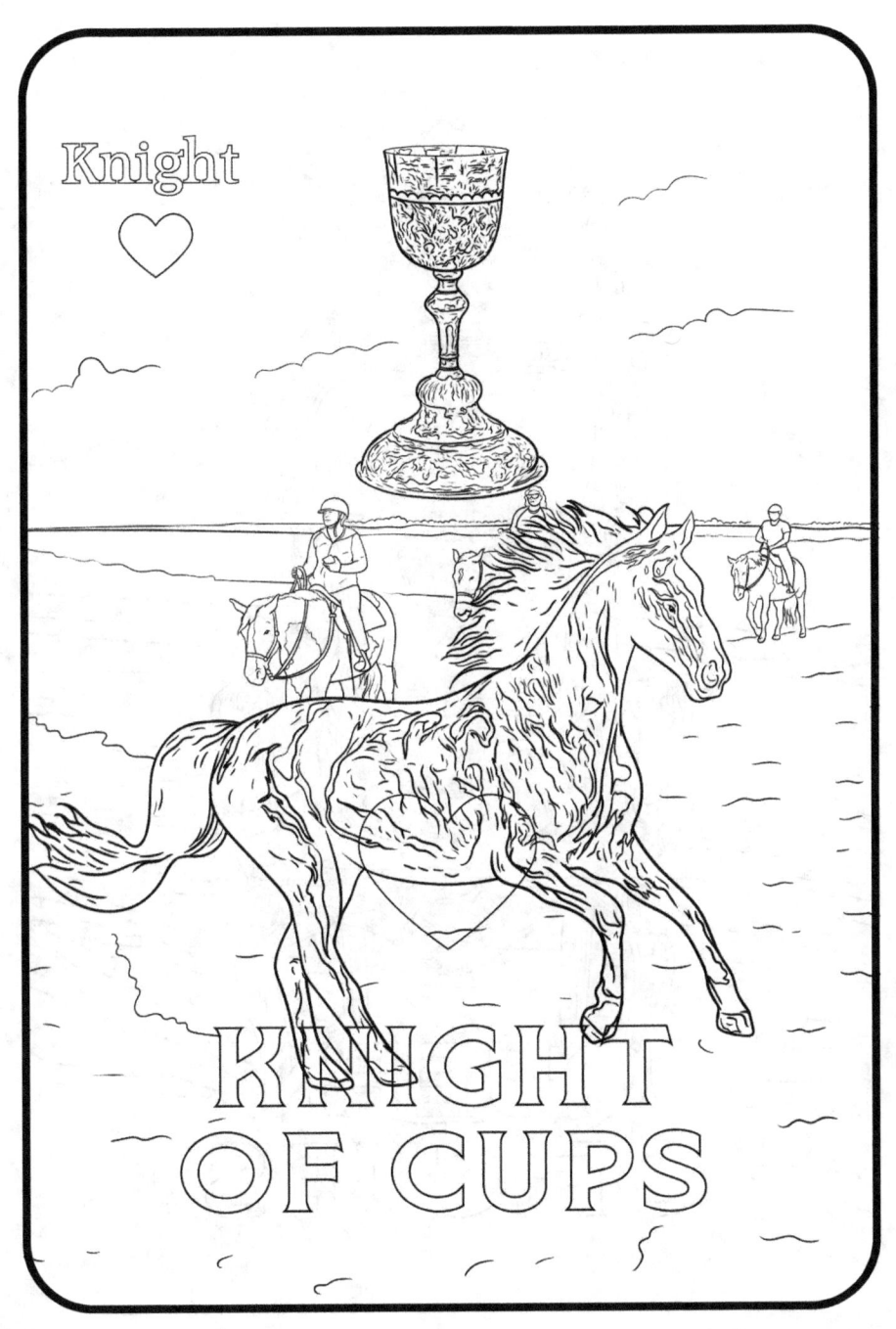

Knight

KNIGHT
OF CUPS

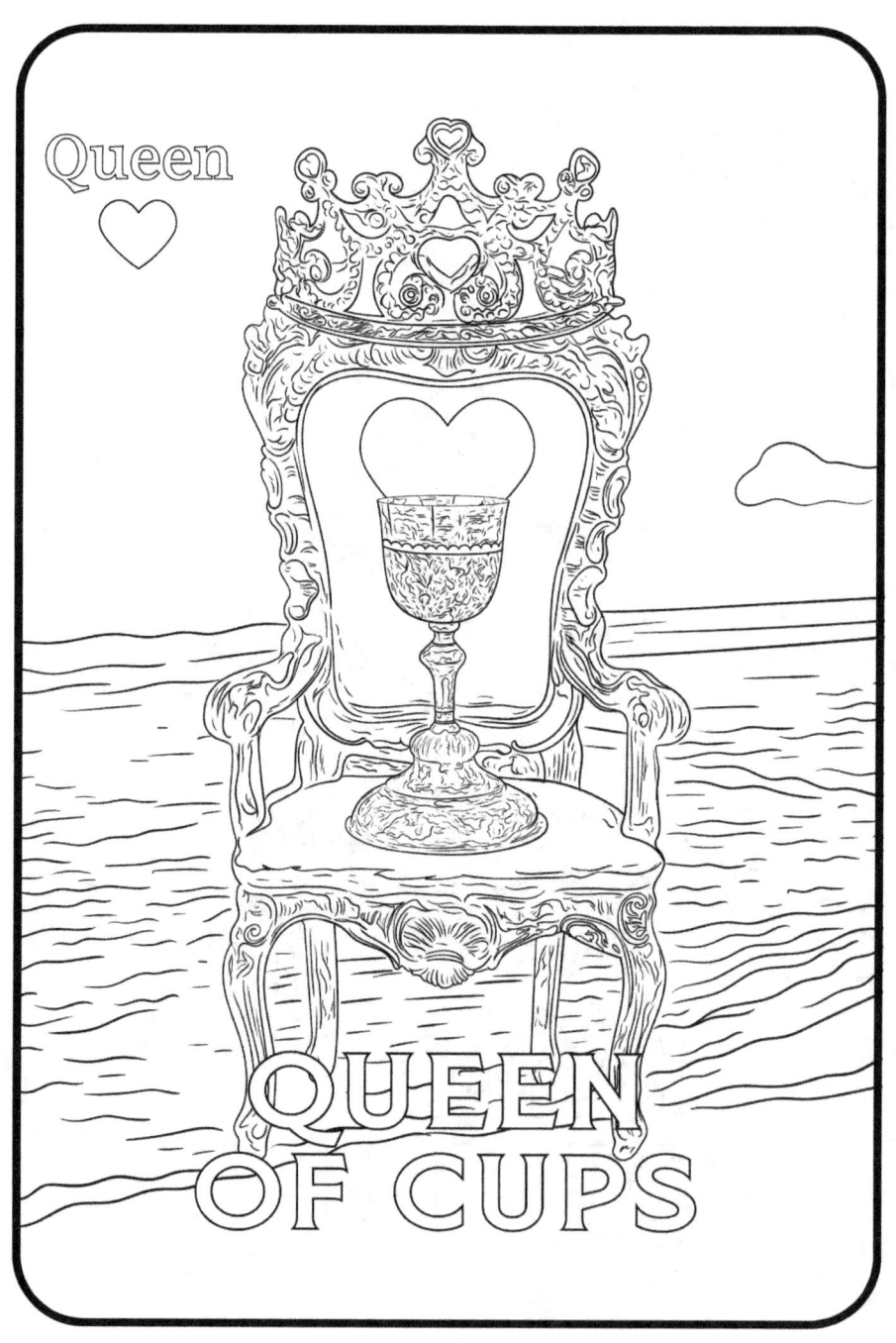

Queen ♡

QUEEN OF CUPS

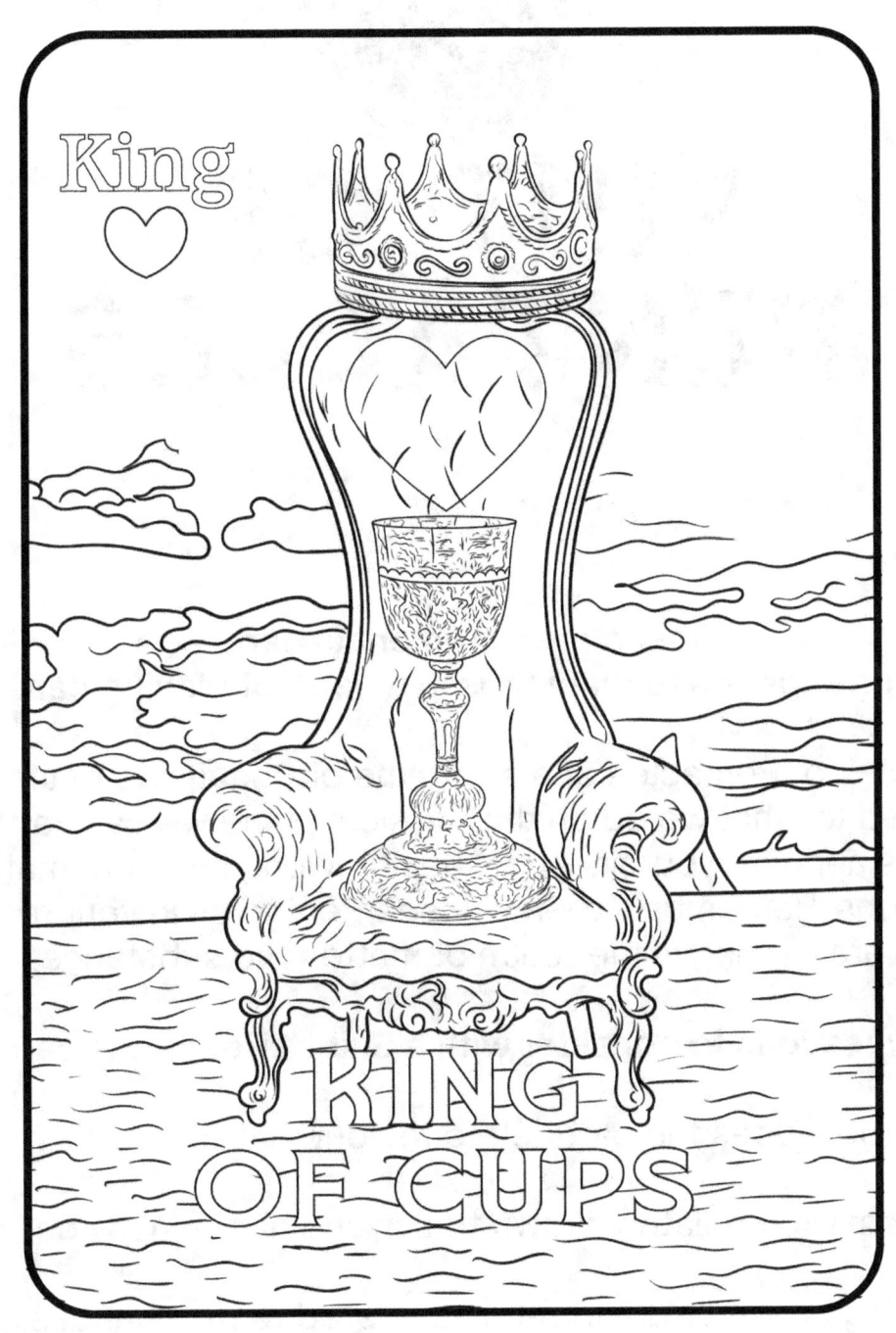

SUIT OF PENTACLES

**Associated element is earth.
Corresponds to diamonds in a deck of playing cards.**

The Suit of Pentacles deals with the physical side of life. It is connected to what we do on the physical plane we call Earth. These cards apply to your finances, health, work, and your material possessions. Remember when you see Pentacles in your reading you are dealing in the realm of matter and substance.

Questions to consider with a Suit of Pentacles card:

How does the card relate to your material world?

What am I immediately drawn to thinking about in my daily life?

Am I being pulled to do something related to my finances, health, or work?

SUIT OF PENTACLES QUICK GUIDE

Ace of Pentacles
Upright: New opportunity, prosperity, and manifestation.

Reversed: Missed chance, bad investment, and lost opportunity.

About the Wandering Traveler card:
My mother's garden in Snohomish, Washington.

Two of Pentacles
Upright: Balancing decisions, prioritization, and adapting.

Reversed: Overwhelmed, unbalanced, and disorganized.

About the Wandering Traveler card:
A funky pink wallet with my two cents in Coeur d'Alene, Idaho.

Three of Pentacles
Upright: Collaboration, teamwork, and learning.

Reversed: Group issues, unhealthy competition, and disorganization.

About the Wandering Traveler card:
My typewriter at my house in Couer d'Alene, Idaho.

Four of Pentacles
Upright: Possessiveness, frugal, and security.

Reversed: Greed, stinginess, and materialism.

About the Wandering Traveler card:
A rooftop bar with a city view of Nashville, Tennessee.

Five of Pentacles
Upright: Poverty, isolation, and worry.

Reversed: Recovery from material loss, charity, and receiving help.

About the Wandering Traveler card:
Way too much snow for Western Washington.

Six of Pentacles
Upright: Perseverance, generosity, and prosperity.

Reversed: Strings attached, debt, and selfishness.

About the Wandering Traveler card:
My favorite treat to bring when you are bribing people to come to a boring work meeting in Everett, Washington.

SUIT OF PENTACLES
QUICK GUIDE

Seven of Pentacles
Upright: Reward, diligence, and perseverance.

Reversed: Lack of growth, failure, and lacking vision.

About the Wandering Traveler card: A city vegetable garden in Seattle, Washington.
.

Eight of Pentacles
Upright: Apprenticeship, education, and passion.

Reversed: Uninspired, lack of ambition, and no motivation.

About the Wandering Traveler card: Learning woodworking in Post Falls, Idaho.

Nine of Pentacles
Upright: Fruits of your labor, reward, and luxury.

Reversed: False success, living beyond your means, and financial setbacks.

About the Wandering Traveler card: The tulip fields in Mount Vernon, Washington.

Ten of Pentacles
Upright: Inheritance, family legacy, and retirement.

Reversed: Fleeting success, loneliness, and no stability.

About the Wandering Traveler card: My neighborhood and home in Coeur d'Alene, Idaho.

Page of Pentacles
Upright: New career, financial opportunity, and ambition.

Reversed: Short-term focus, lack of commitment, and laziness.

About the Wandering Traveler card: Dusk in the hills of Sedona, Arizona.

Knight of Pentacles
Upright: Hard work, responsible, and efficient.

Reversed: Lazy, unproductive, and careless.

About the Wandering Traveler card: Thoroughbred farm in Ocala, Florida.

SUIT OF PENTACLES
QUICK GUIDE

Queen of Pentacles
Upright: Practical, motherly, and security.

Reversed: Smothering, lack of family, work, life balance, and self-centered.

About the Wandering Traveler card: Admiring the fall leaves right before a pumpkin patch visit in Maltby, Washington.

King of Pentacles
Upright: Prosperity, security, and power

Reversed: Domineering, greed, and indulgence.

About the Wandering Traveler card: The vineyards in Walla Walla, Washington.

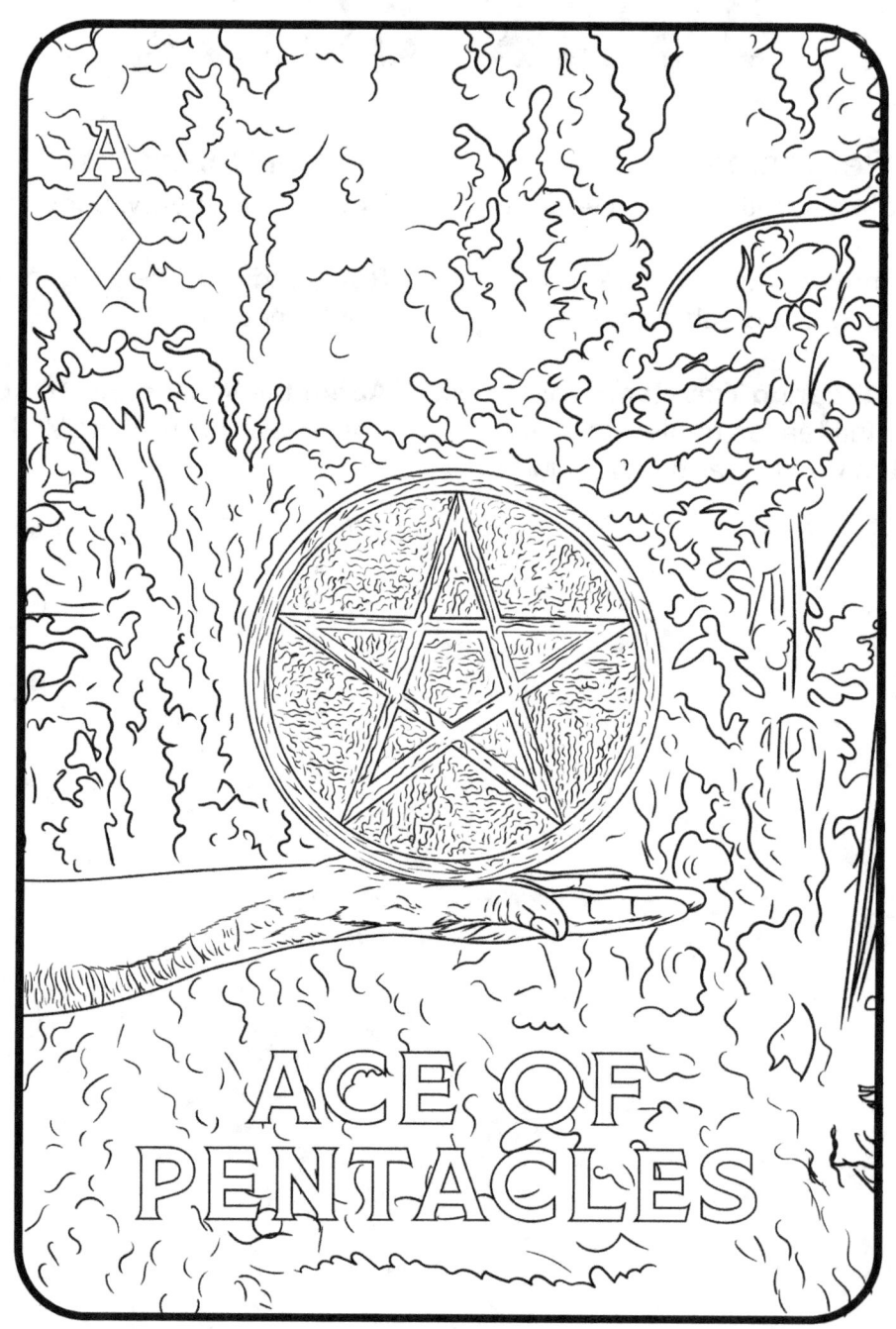

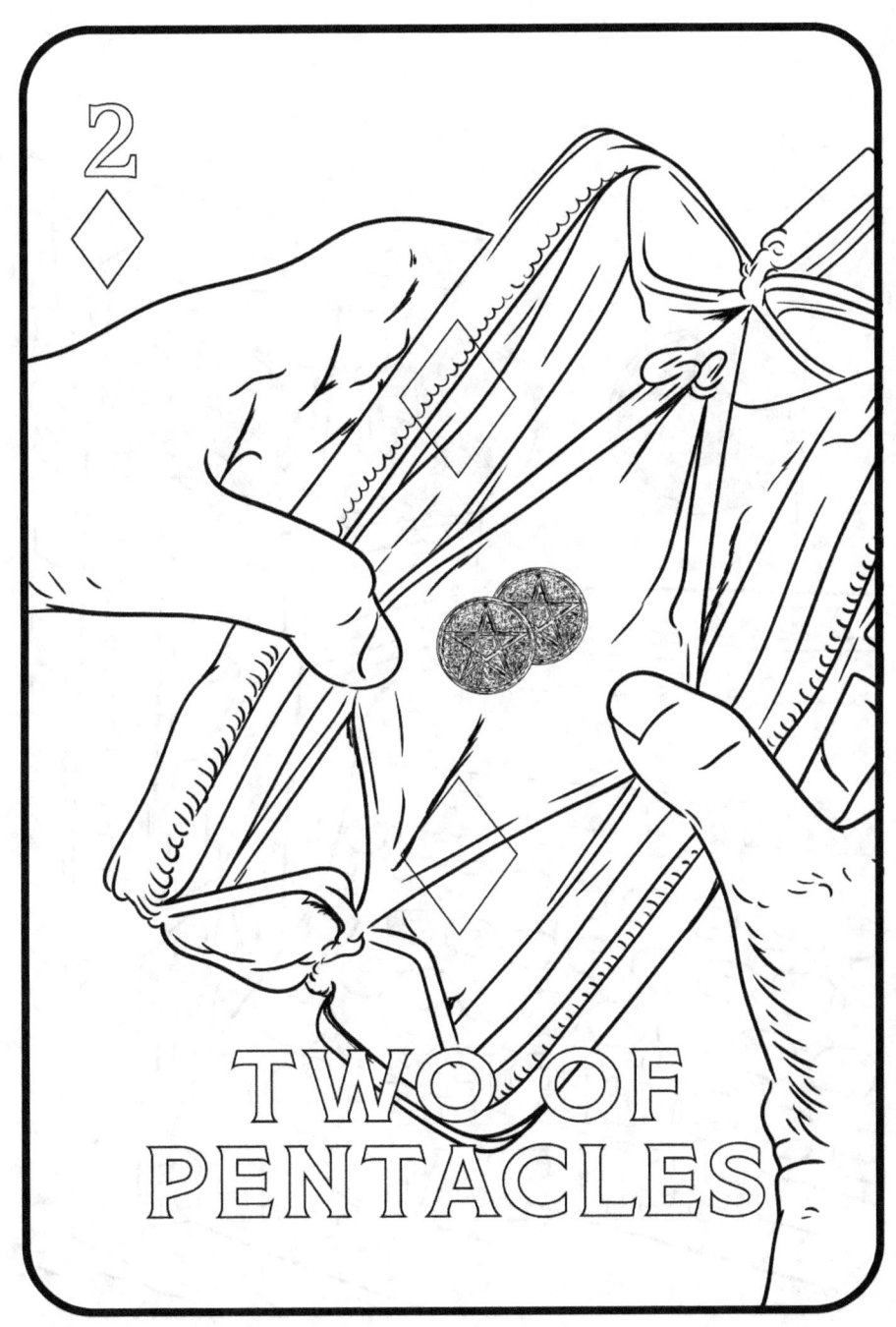

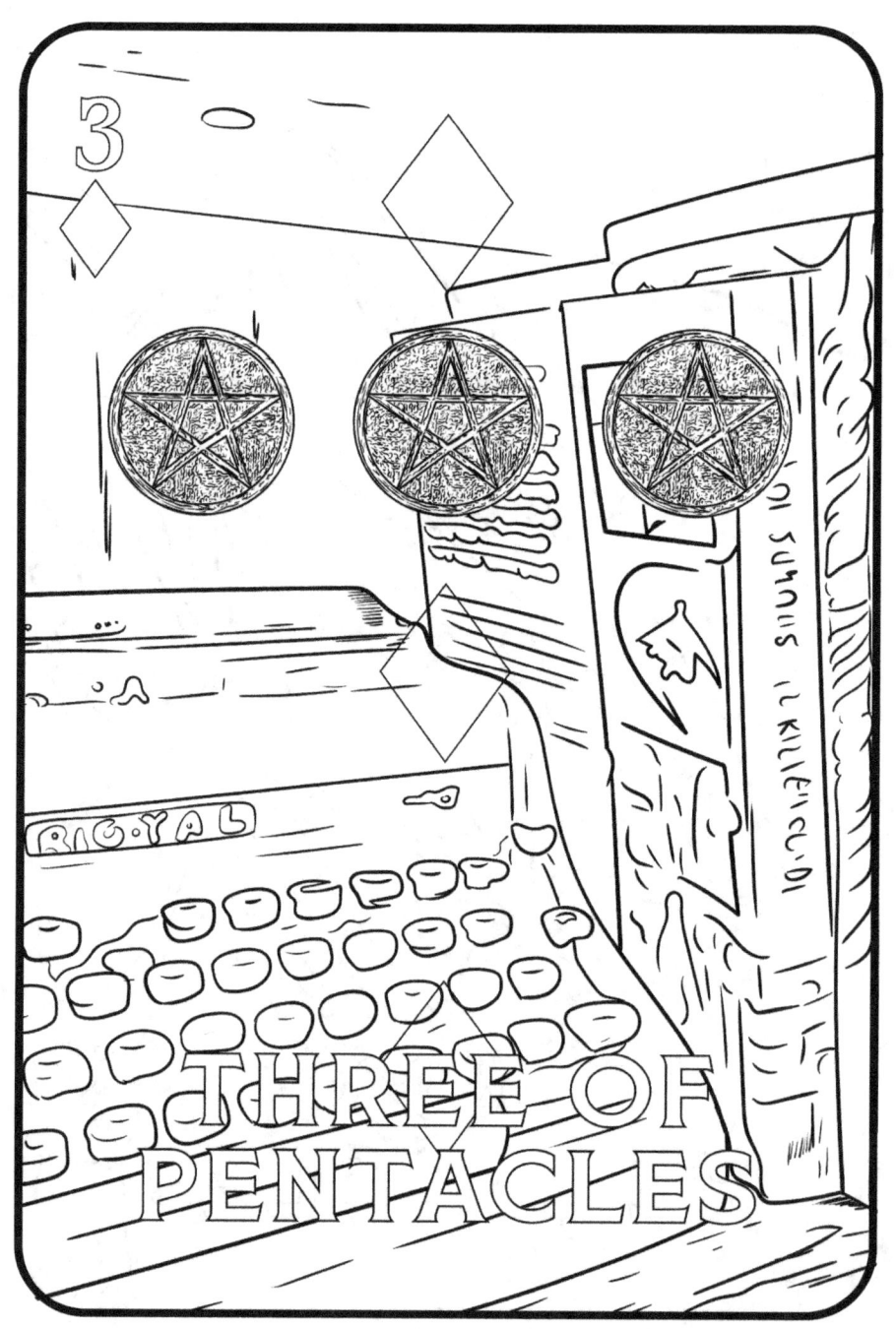

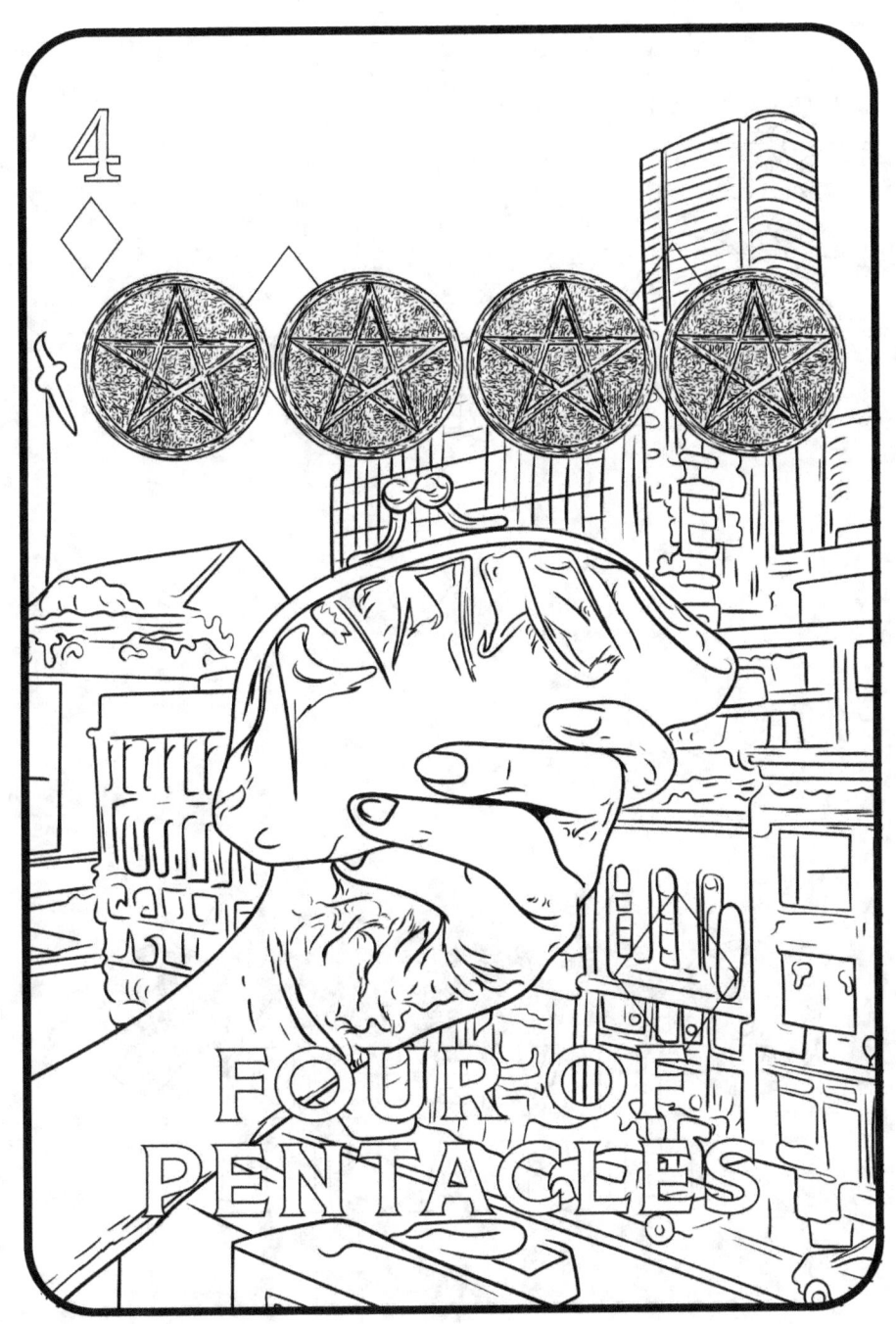

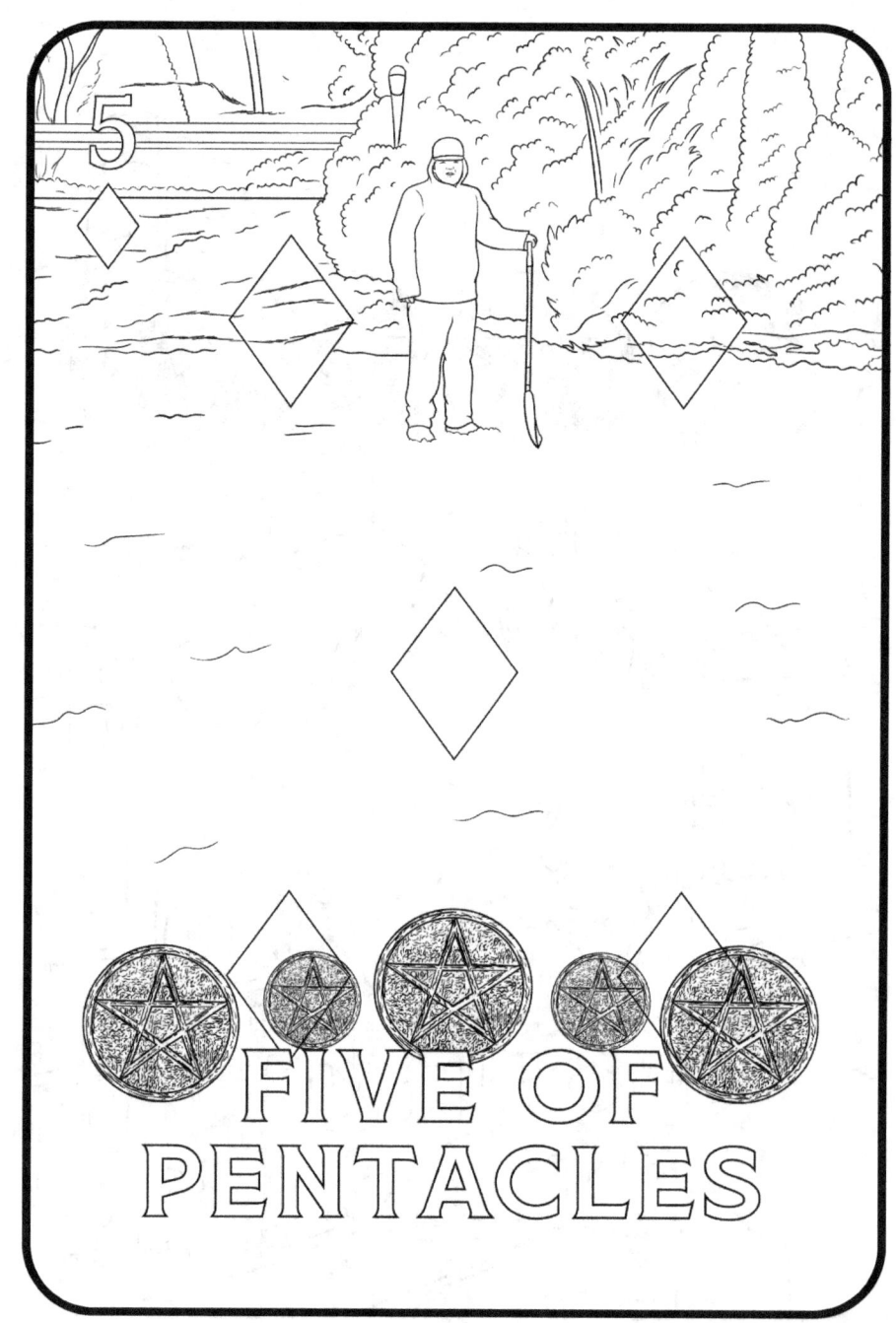

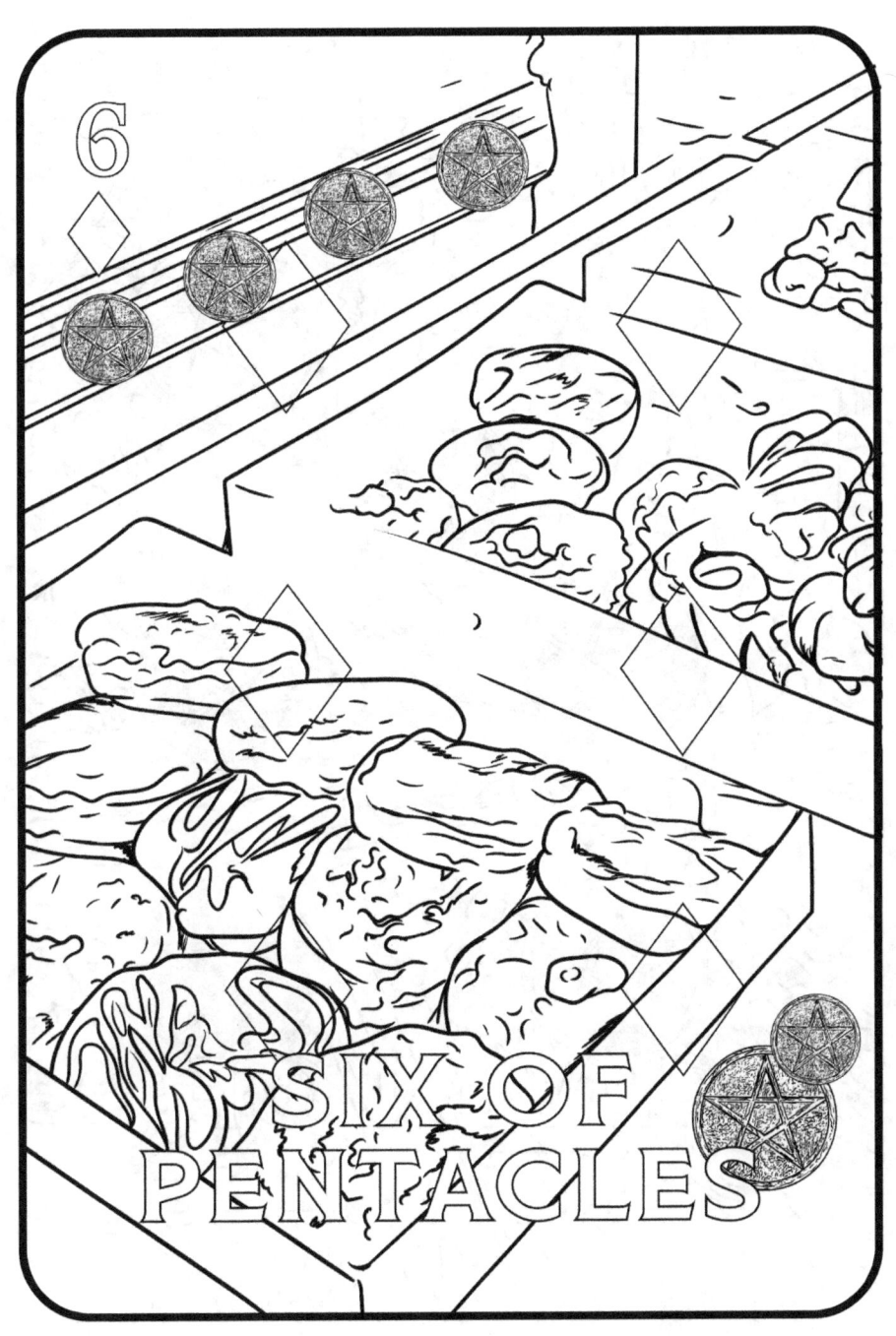

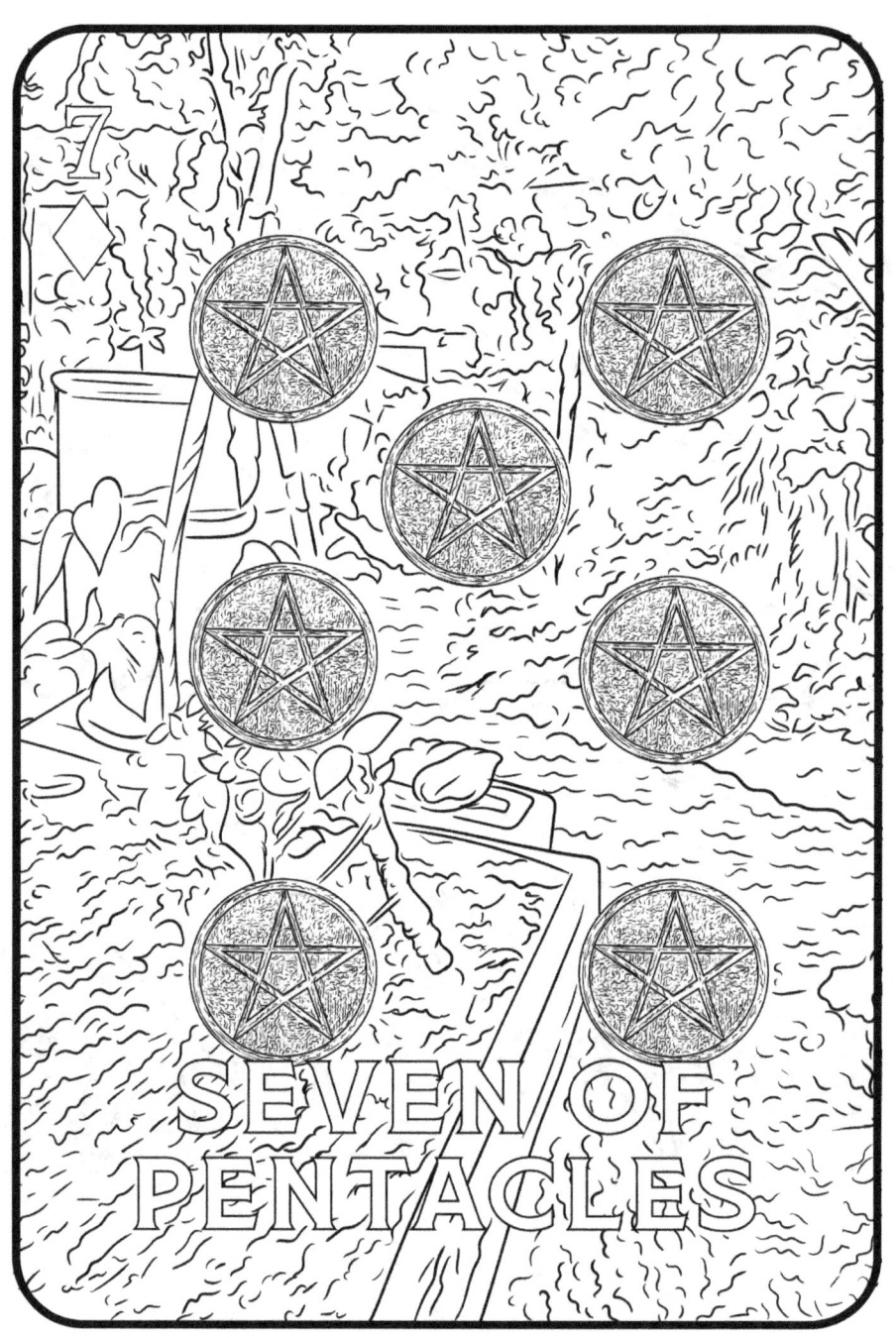

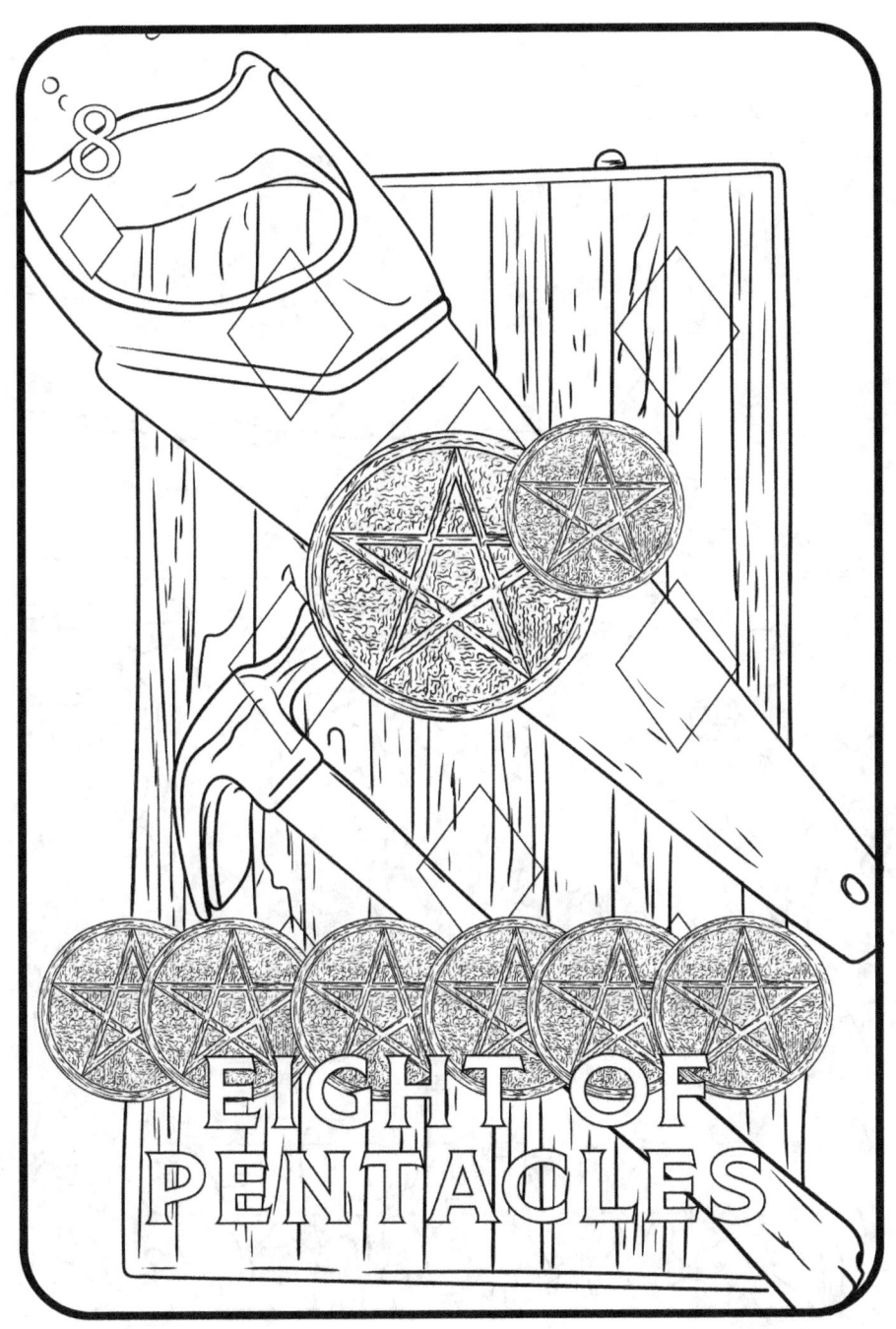

EIGHT OF PENTACLES

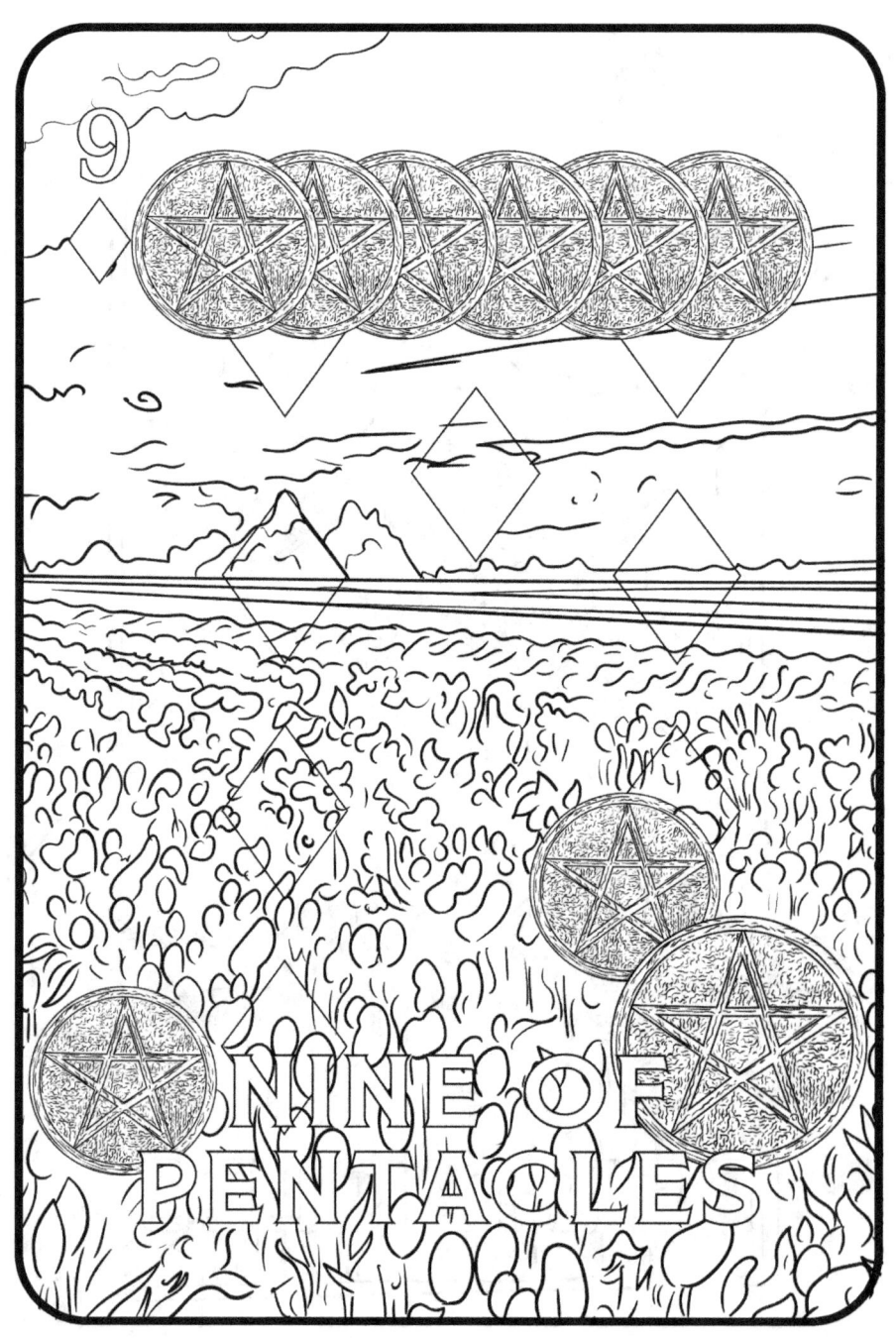

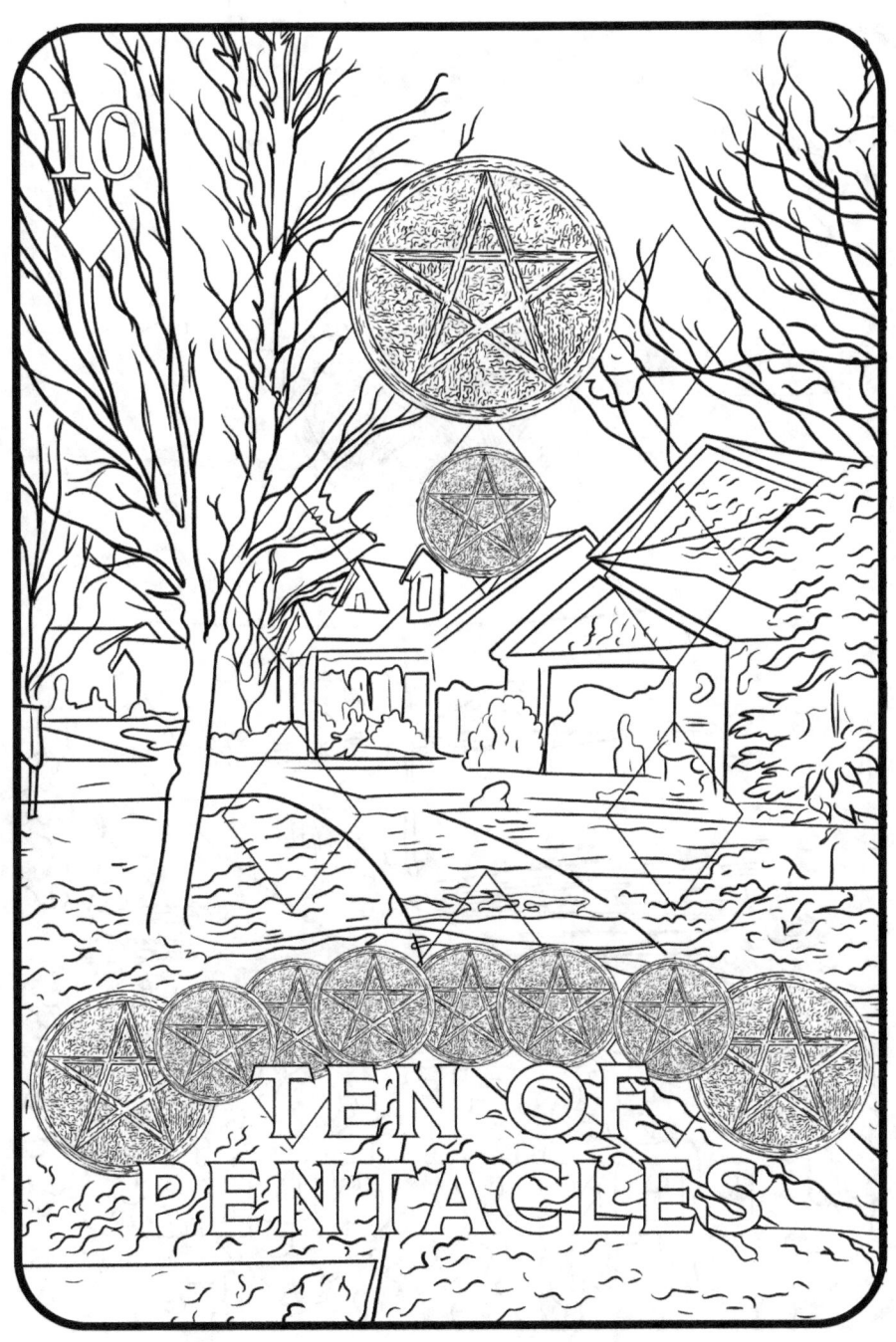

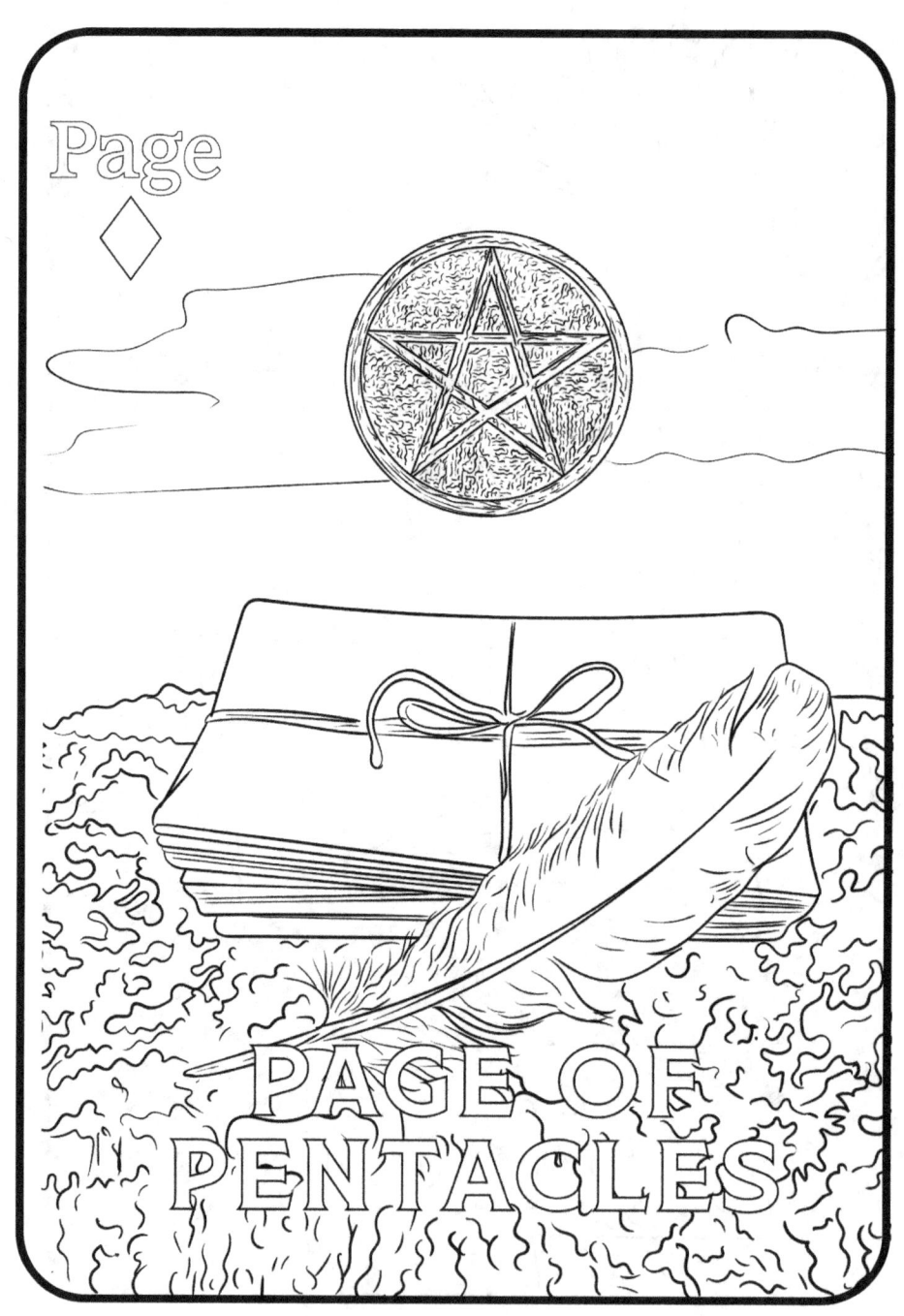

Page ◇

PAGE OF PENTACLES

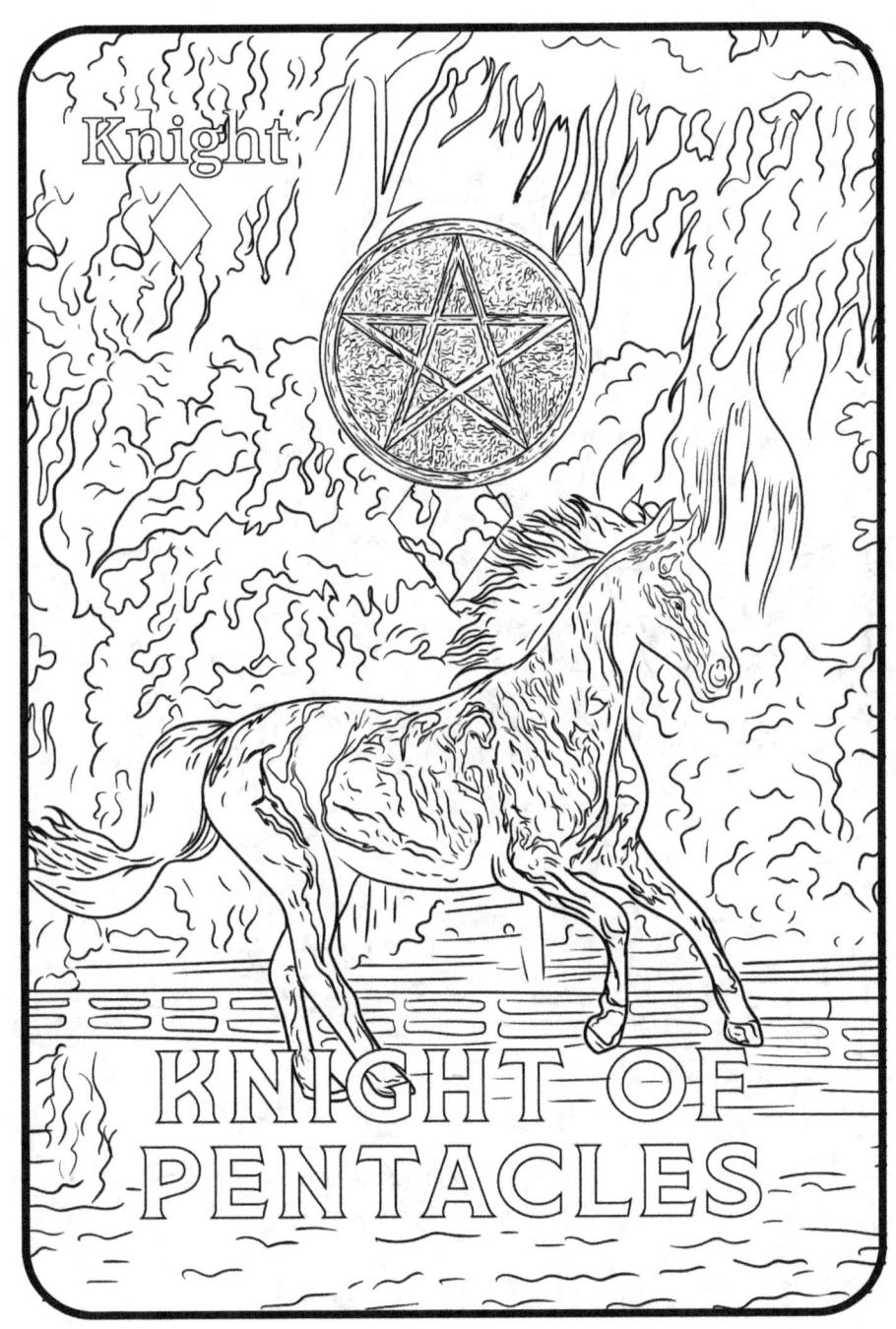

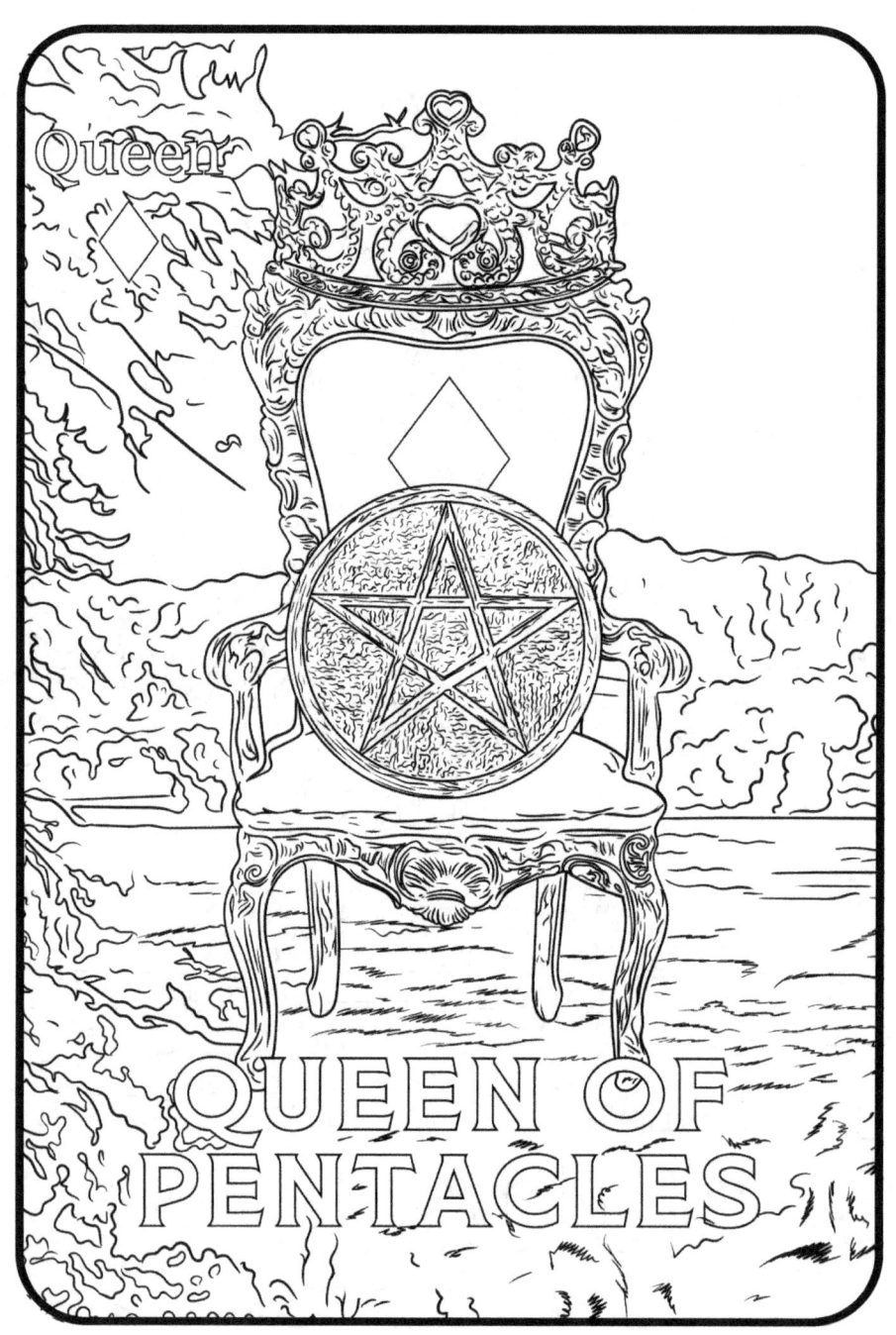

QUEEN OF
PENTACLES

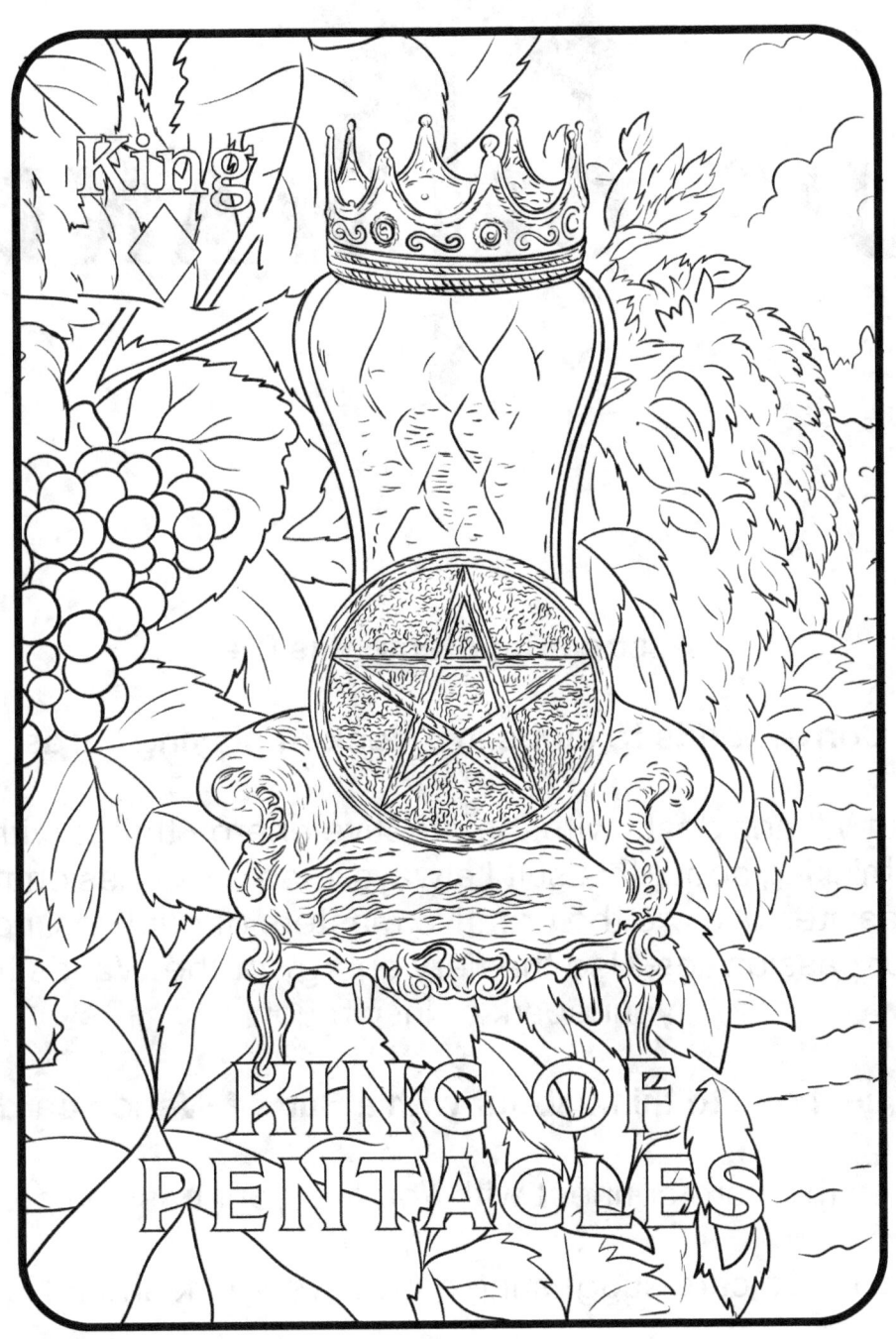

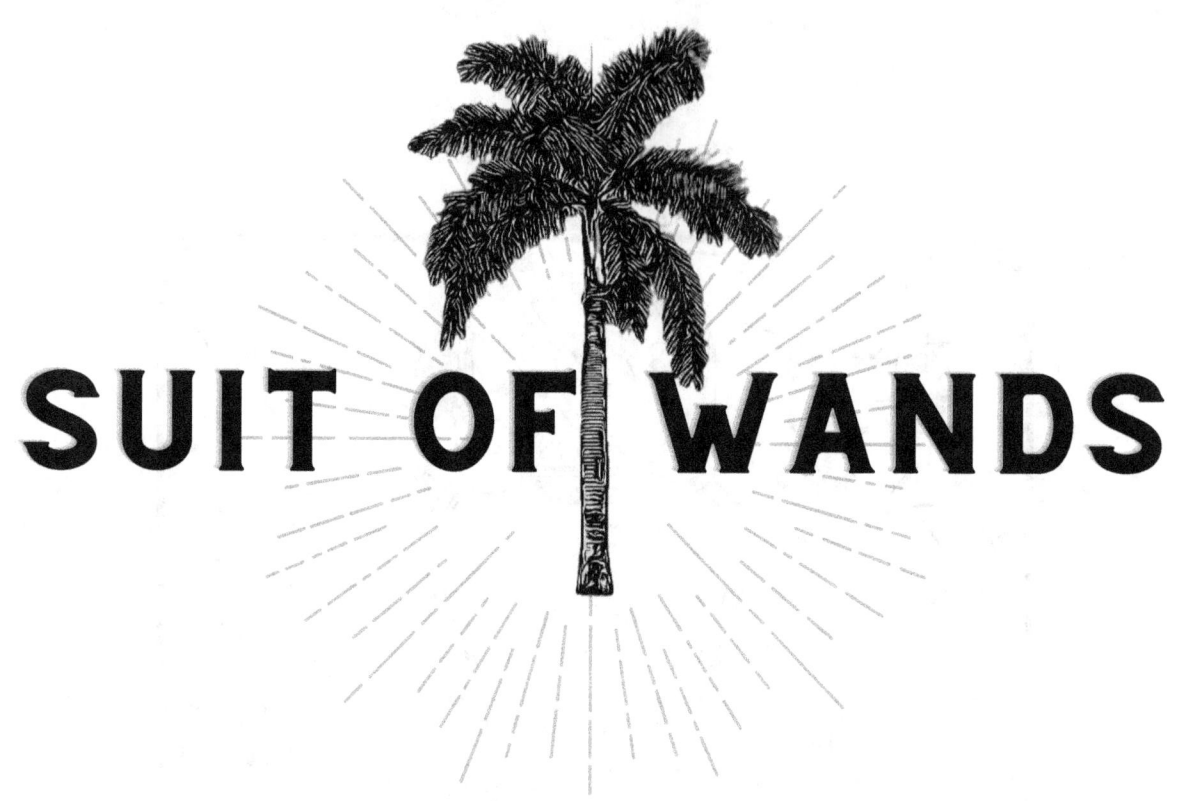

SUIT OF WANDS

Associated element is fire.

Corresponds to clubs in a deck of playing cards.

The Suit of Wands deals with the creative energy that is within us all. When thinking about this suit I always imagine a passionate and volatile painter. We are the creative masters of our lives, no matter where our passion lies. Use the fiery energy of the Wands to propel your spark of inspiration!

Questions to think about with a Suit of Wands card:

How does this card connect with you and your passion projects?

Where is this card suggesting a creative spark should ignite?

Is there anything blocking a current creation-in-progress?

SUIT OF WANDS
QUICK GUIDE

Ace of Wands
Upright: Creation, willpower, and desire.

Reversed: Lack of energy, burnt out, and boredom.

About the Wandering Traveler card: Looking over Los Angeles in the Hollywood Hills of California.

Two of Wands
Upright: Future planning, discovery, and leaving home.

Reversed: Fear of change, lack of planning, and playing it safe.

About the Wandering Traveler card: Old city gates in St. Augustine, Florida.

Three of Wands
Upright: Foresight, rapid growth, and expansion.

Reversed: Delays, obstacles, and frustration.

About the Wandering Traveler card: Sailing under the Golden Gate Bridge in San Francisco, California.

Four of Wands
Upright: Celebration, community, and harmony.

Reversed: Lack of community, conflicts at home, and without a home.

About the Wandering Traveler card: The Oak Alley Plantation house in Vacherie, Louisiana.

Five of Wands
Upright: Rivalry, conflict, and disagreement.

Reversed: Avoiding conflict, respect, and mutual understanding.

About the Wandering Traveler card: Looking into a bonfire in Chattaroy, Washington.

Six of Wands
Upright: Public recognition, victory, and success.

Reversed: Egotism, lack of recognition, and fall from grace.

About the Wandering Traveler card: Concert time in Austin, Texas.

SUIT OF WANDS
QUICK GUIDE

Seven of Wands

Upright: Perseverance, challenge, and competition.

Reversed: Giving up, overwhelmed, and ruined confidence.

About the Wandering Traveler card: Cliff dwelling ruins at Palatki Heritage Site in Sedona, Arizona.

Eight of Wands

Upright: Air travel, fast action, and swift change.

Reversed: Delays, waiting, and holding off.

About the Wandering Traveler card: Final landing into Los Angeles, California.

Nine of Wands

Upright: Test of faith, persistence, and resilience.

Reversed: Exhaustion, hesitant, and giving up.

About the Wandering Traveler card: Wine Safari in the hills of Malibu, California.

Ten of Wands

Upright: Burden, responsibility, and hard work.

Reversed: Taking on too much, avoiding work, and overstressed.

About the Wandering Traveler card: Moon circle night with friends in Marysville, Washington.

Page of Wands

Upright: Exploration, enthusiasm, and free spirit.

Reversed: Lack of direction, procrastination, and melancholy.

About the Wandering Traveler card: Flying kites at Ocean Shores, Washington.

Knight of Wands

Upright: Impulsive, lust, and fearlessness.

Reversed: Anger, impulsive, and reckless.

About the Wandering Traveler card: The practice track in Ocala, Florida.

SUIT OF WANDS
QUICK GUIDE

Queen of Wands

Upright: Vibrancy, warmth, and exuberance.

Reversed: Insecurities, boring, and unfeeling.

About the Wandering Traveler card:
A Tropicana rose in Snohomish, Washington.

King of Wands

Upright: Leader, honor, and entrepreneur.

Reversed: High expectations, overbearing, and impulsive.

About the Wandering Traveler card:
Palm trees blowing in the wind at Kualoa Regional Park in Honolulu, Hawaii.

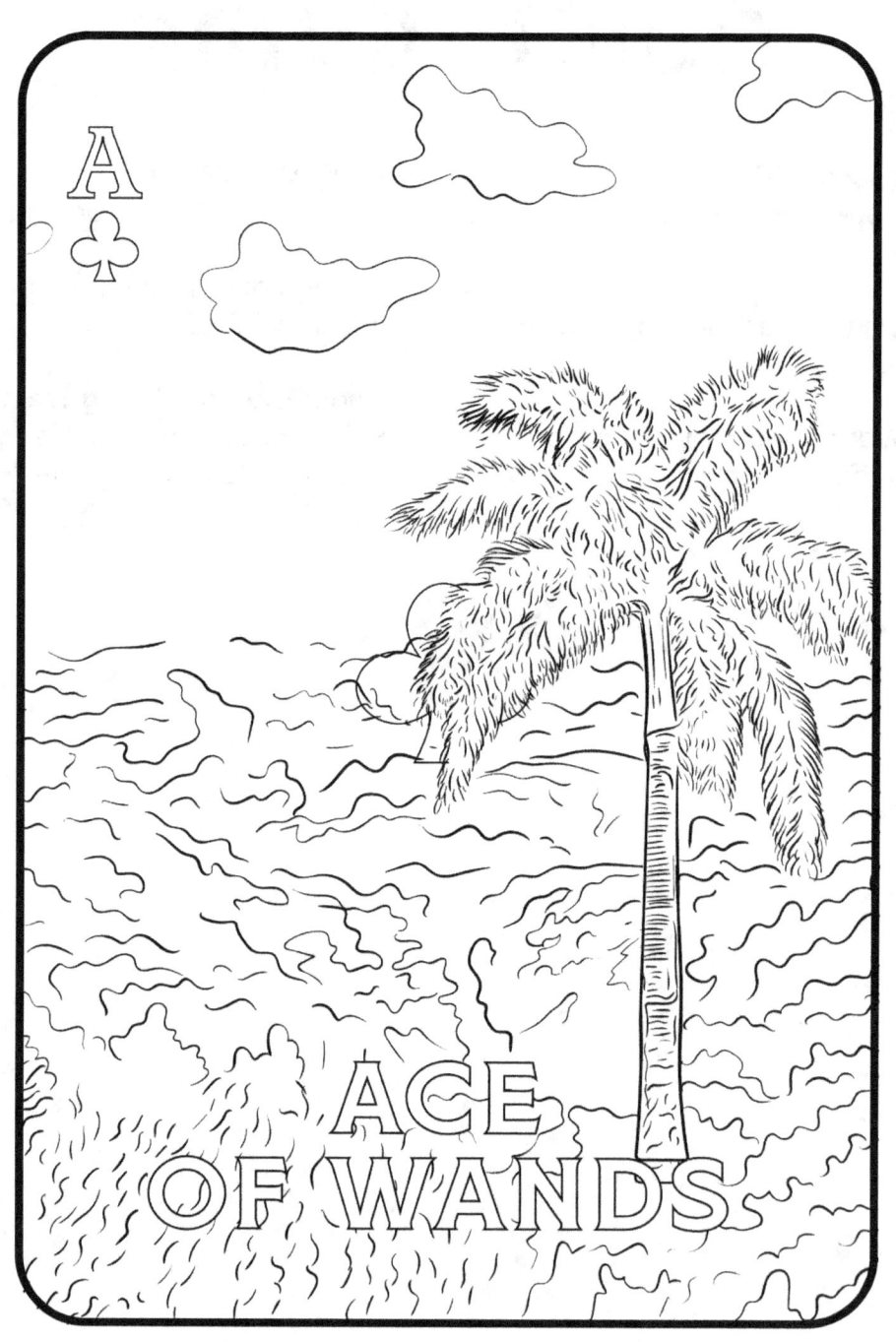

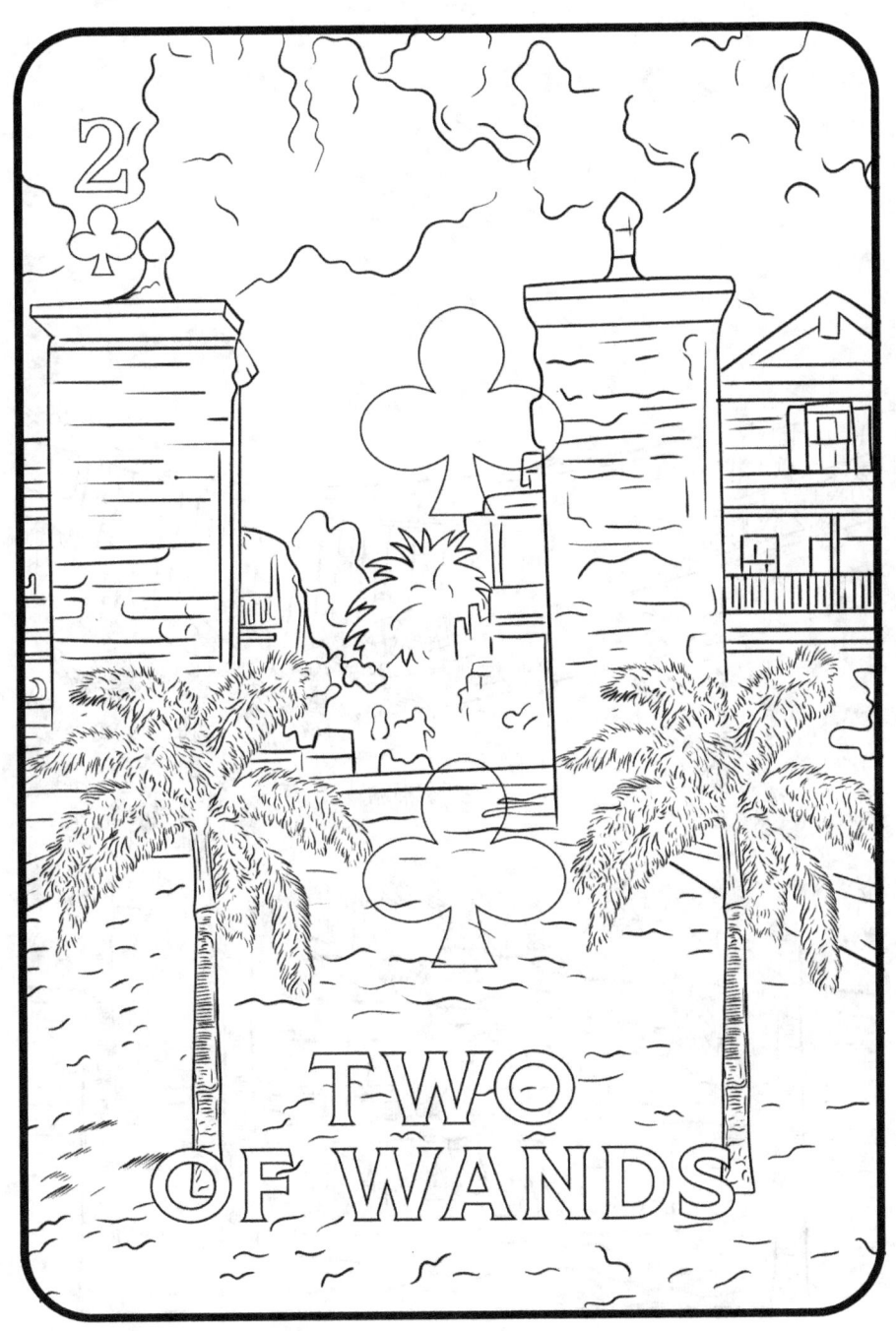

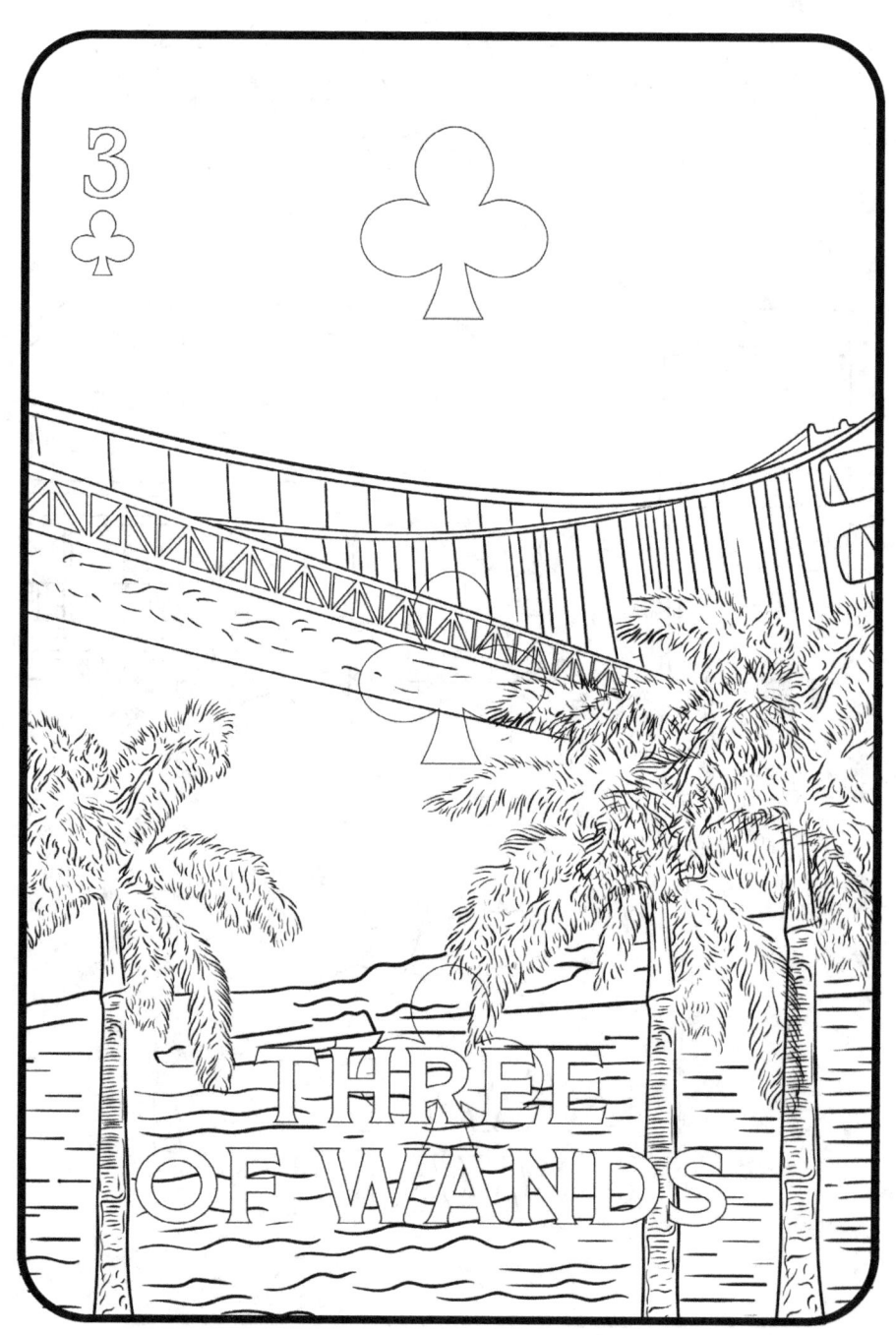

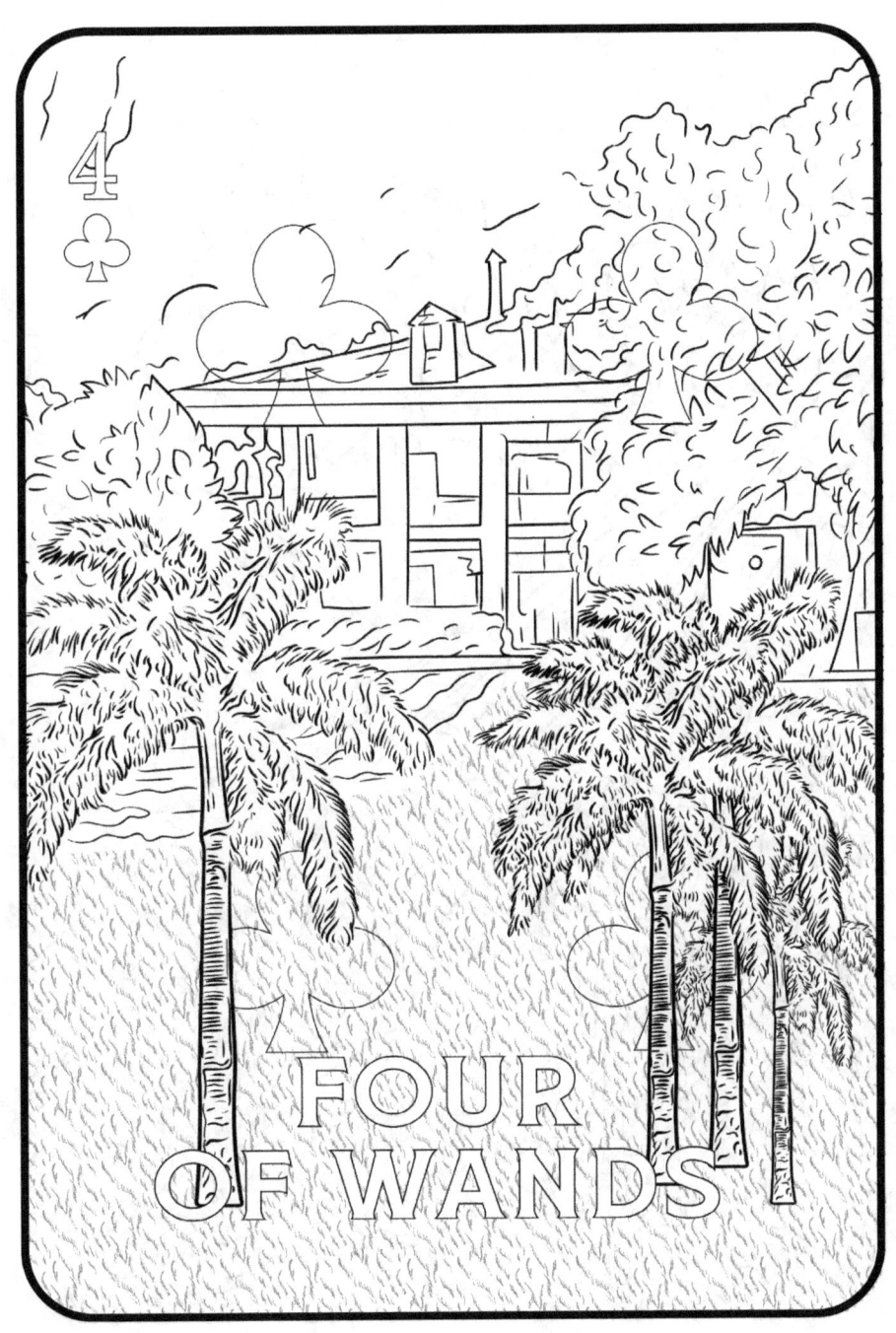

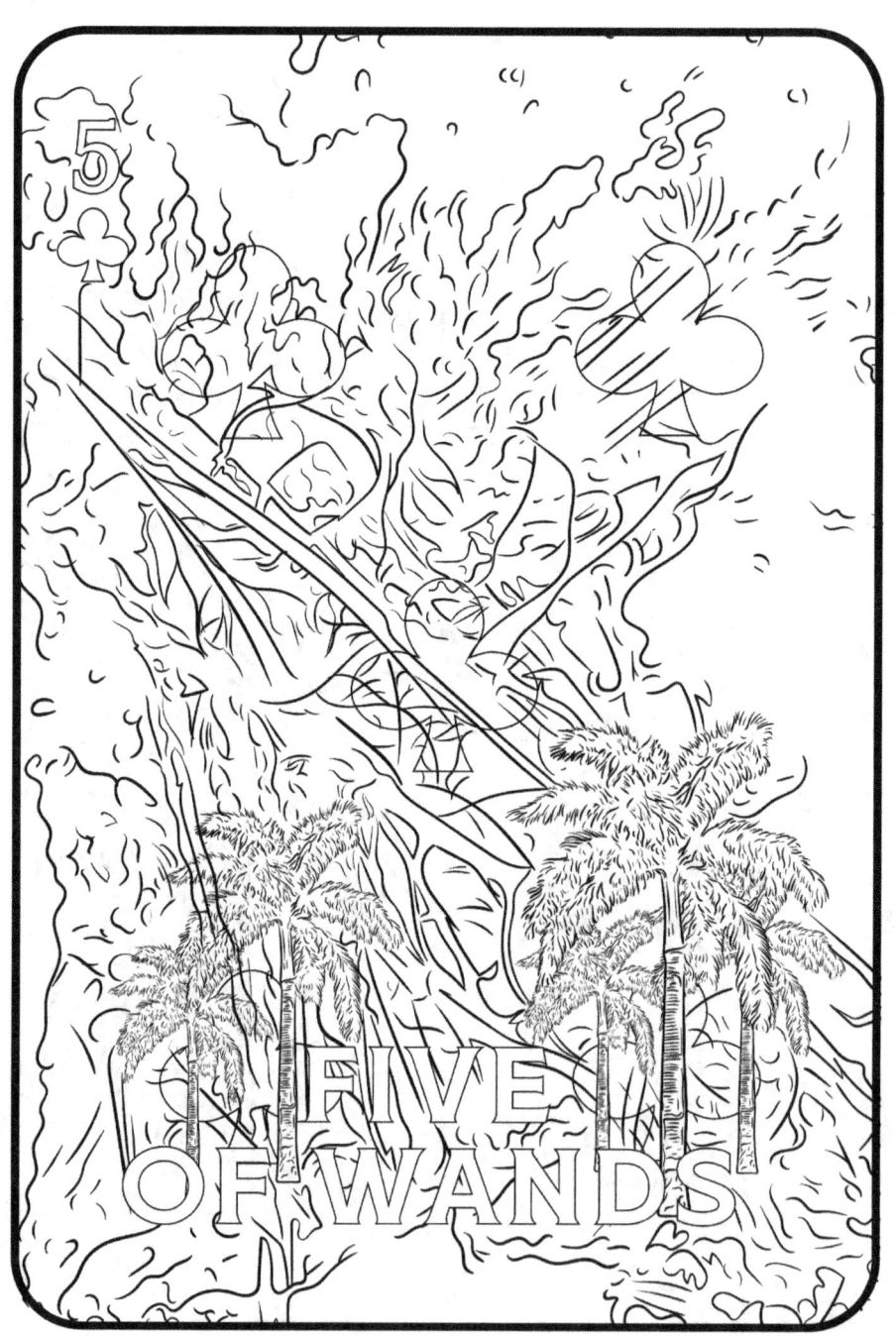

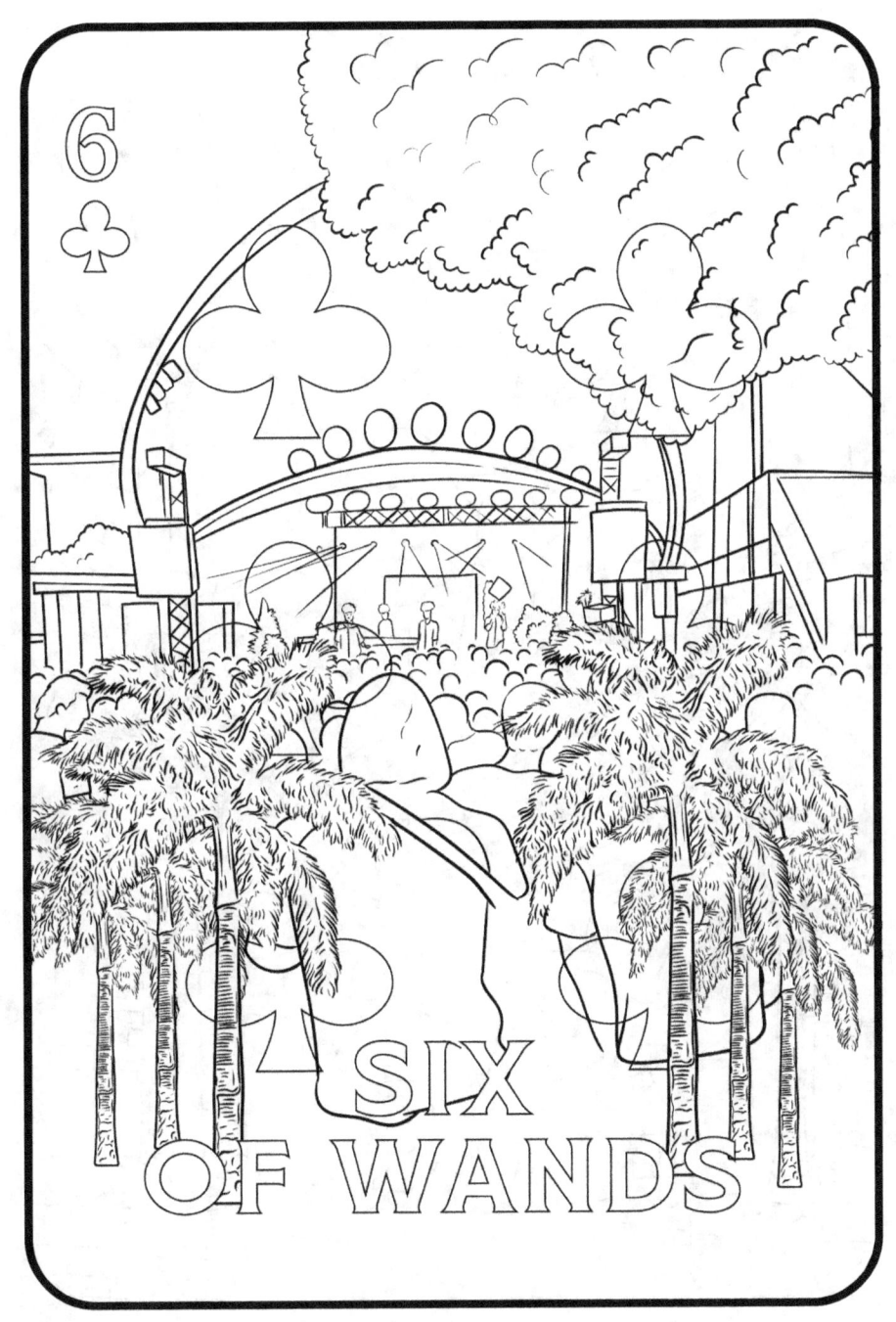

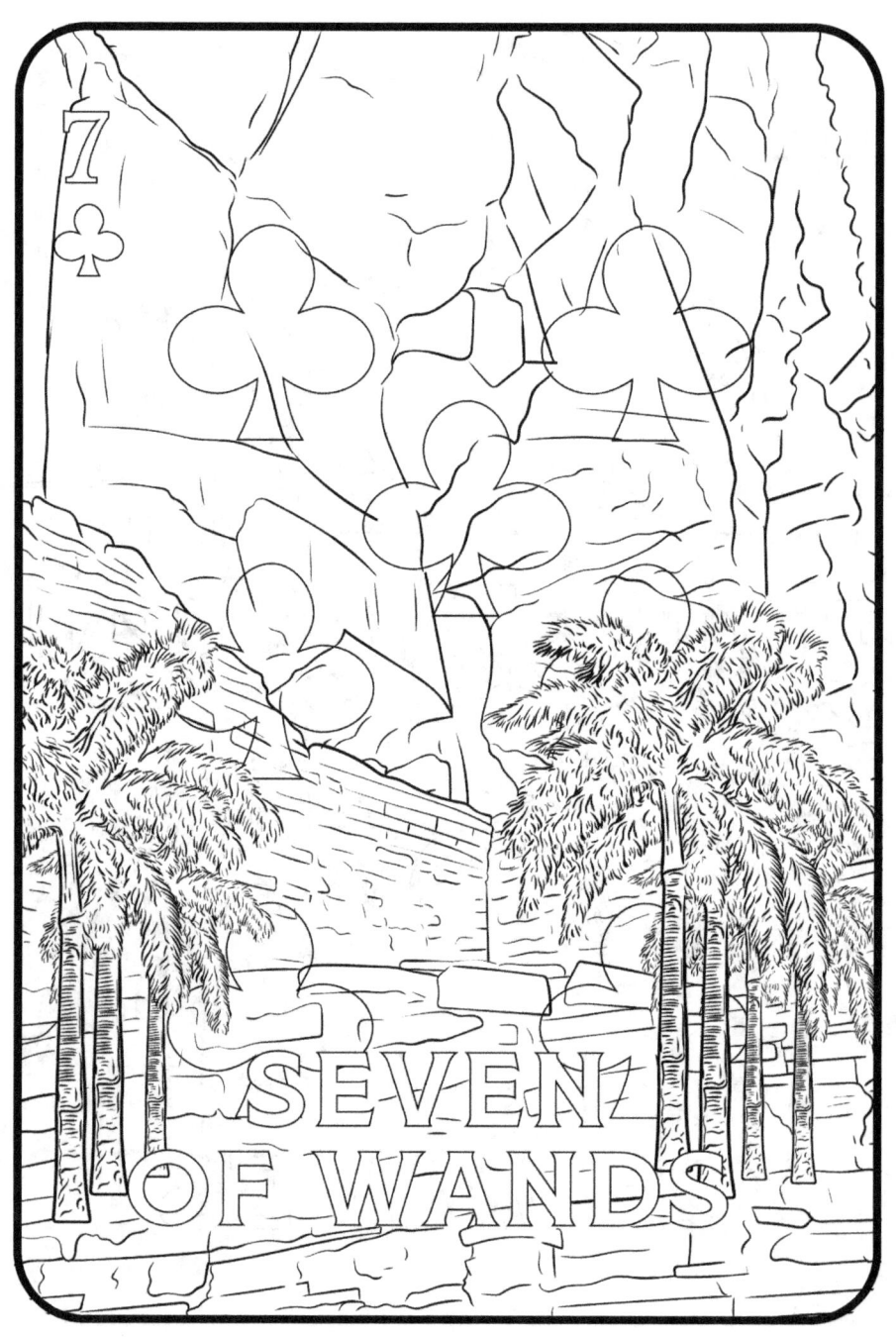

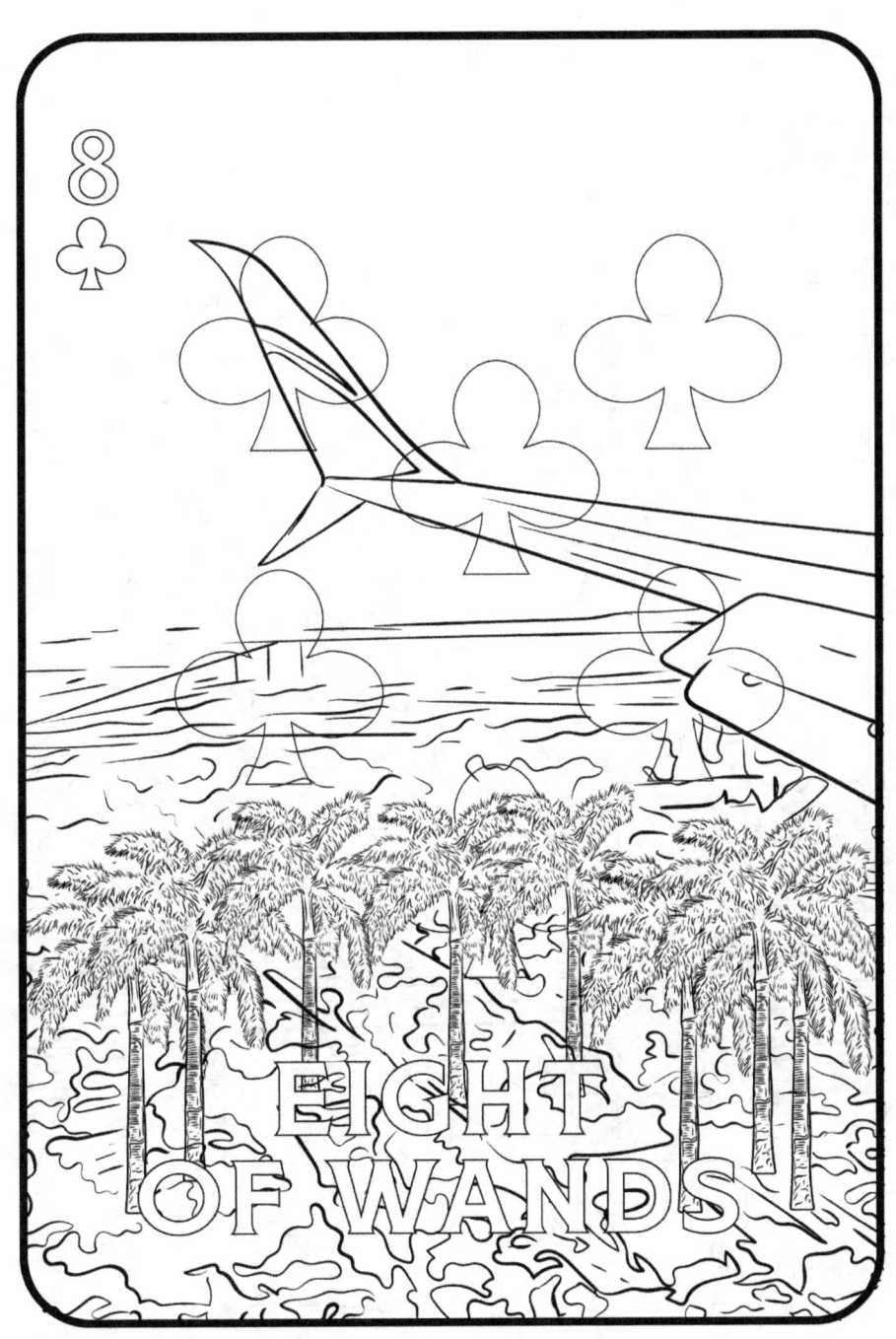

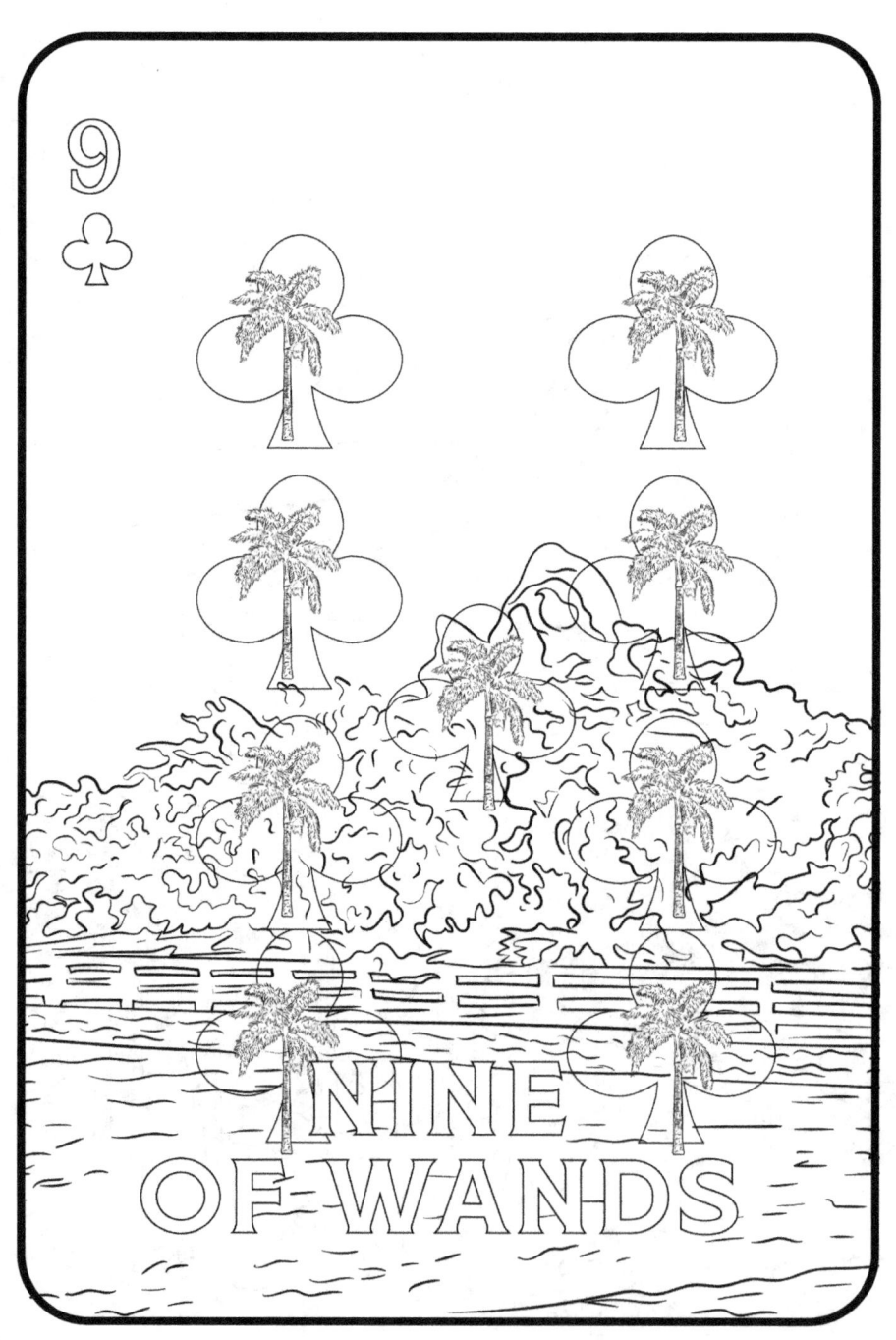

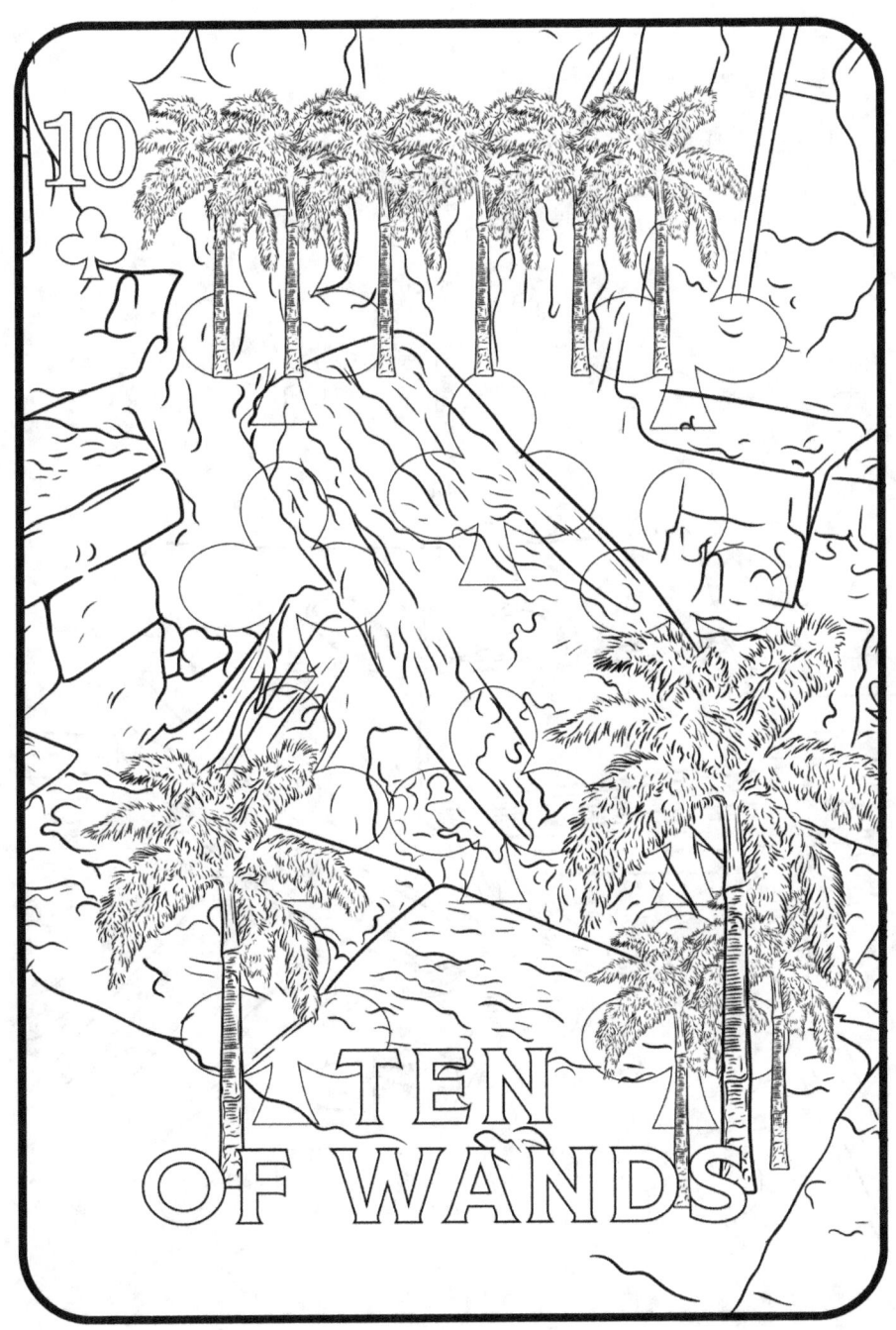

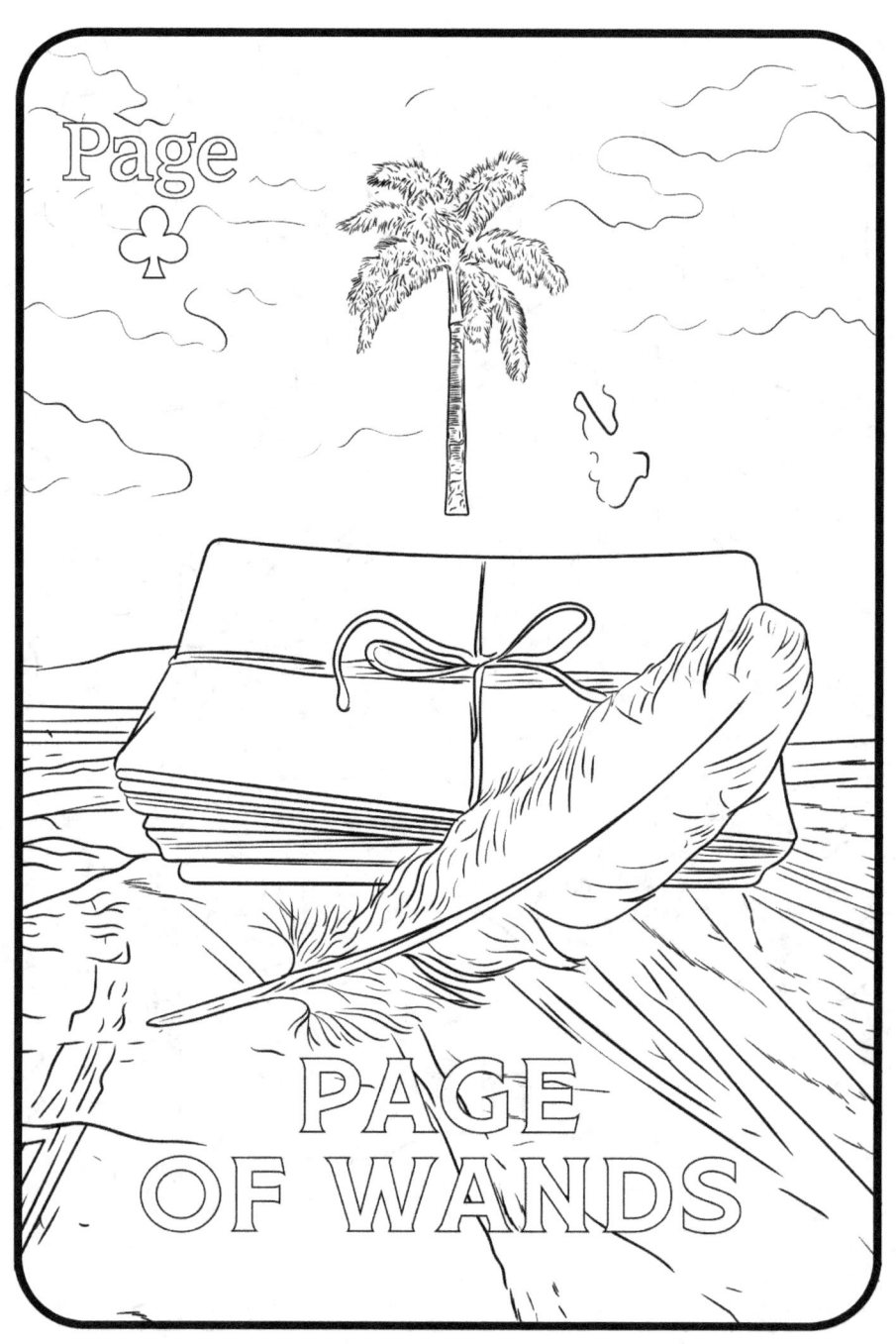

Page ♣

PAGE
OF WANDS

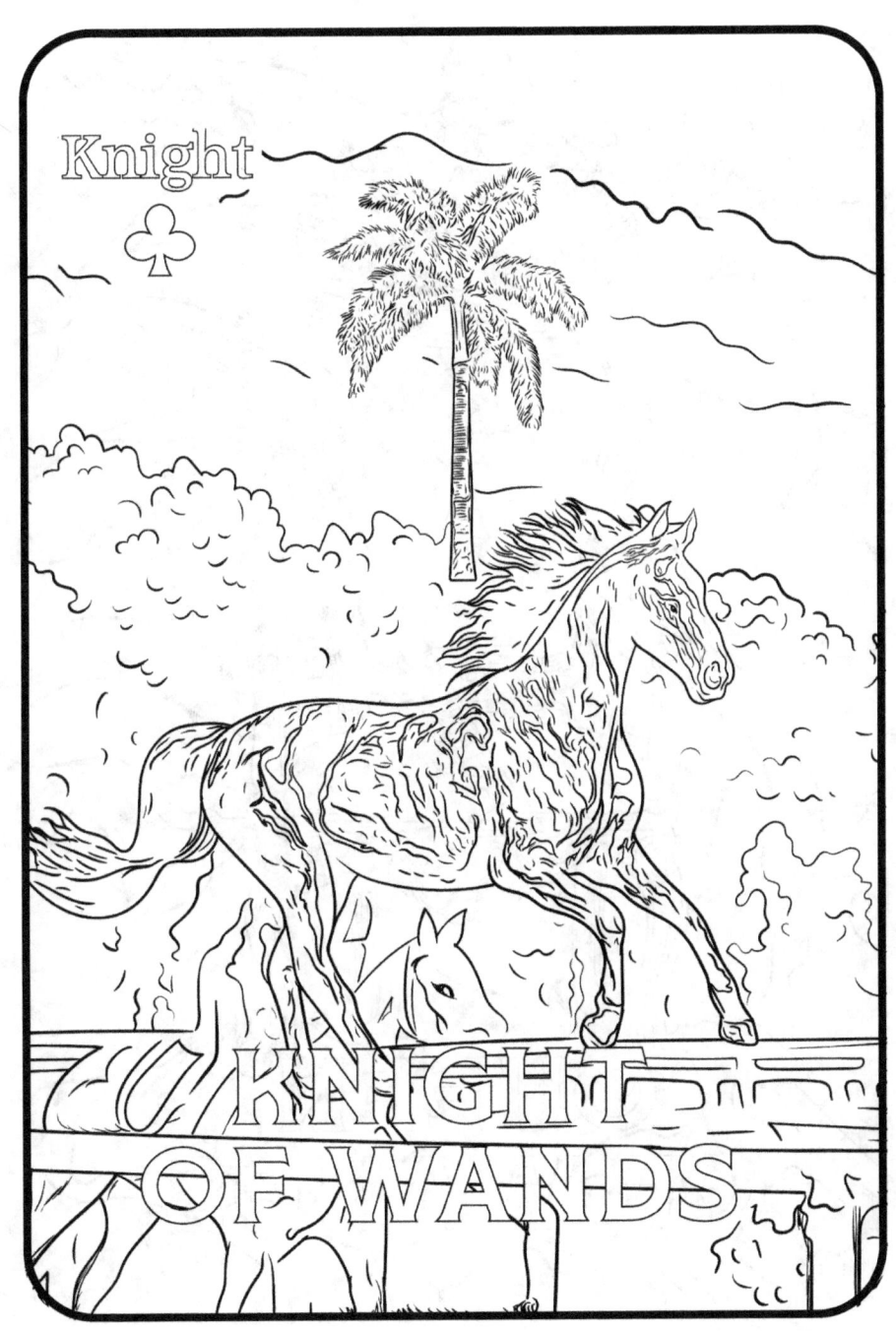

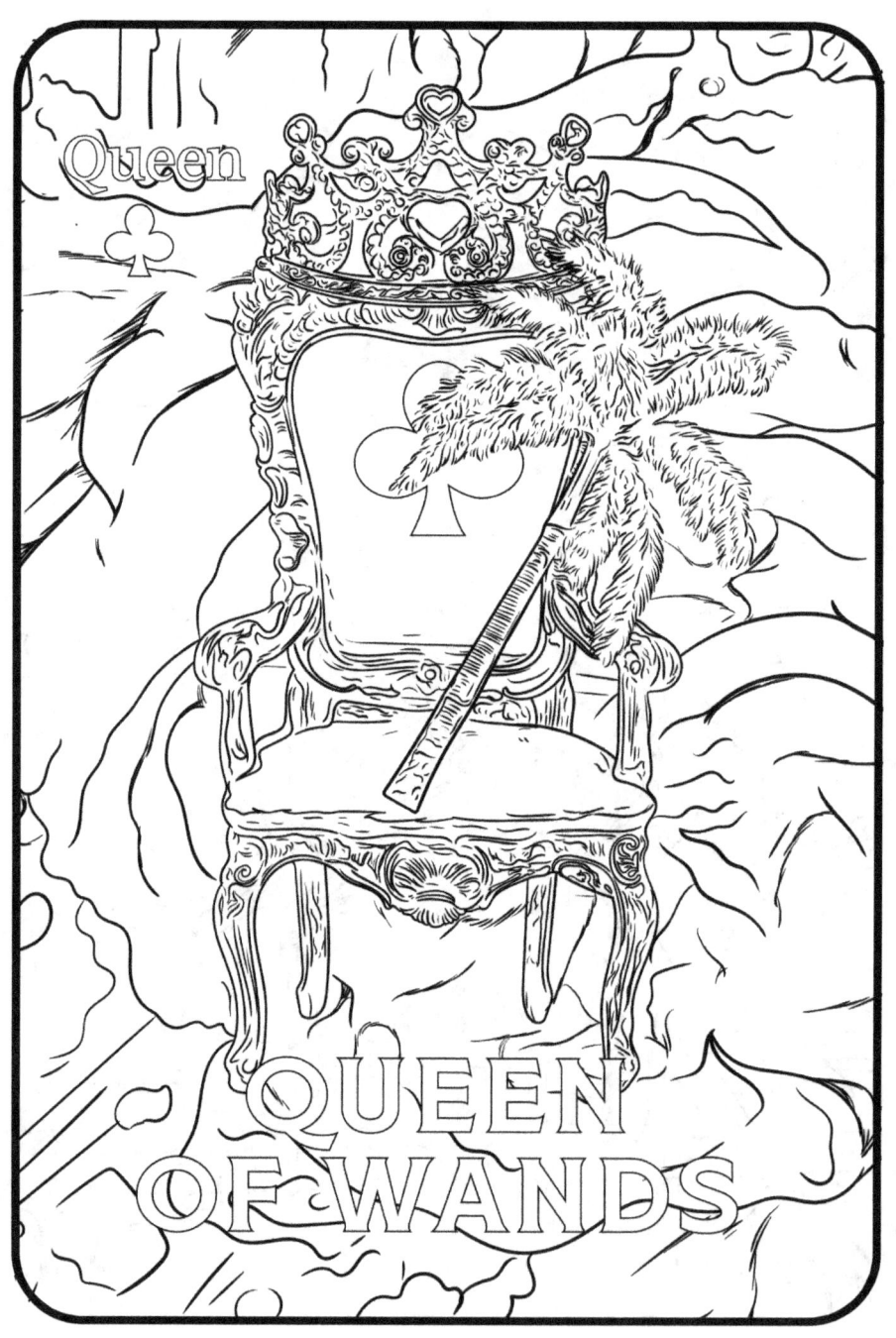

Queen

♣

QUEEN
OF WANDS

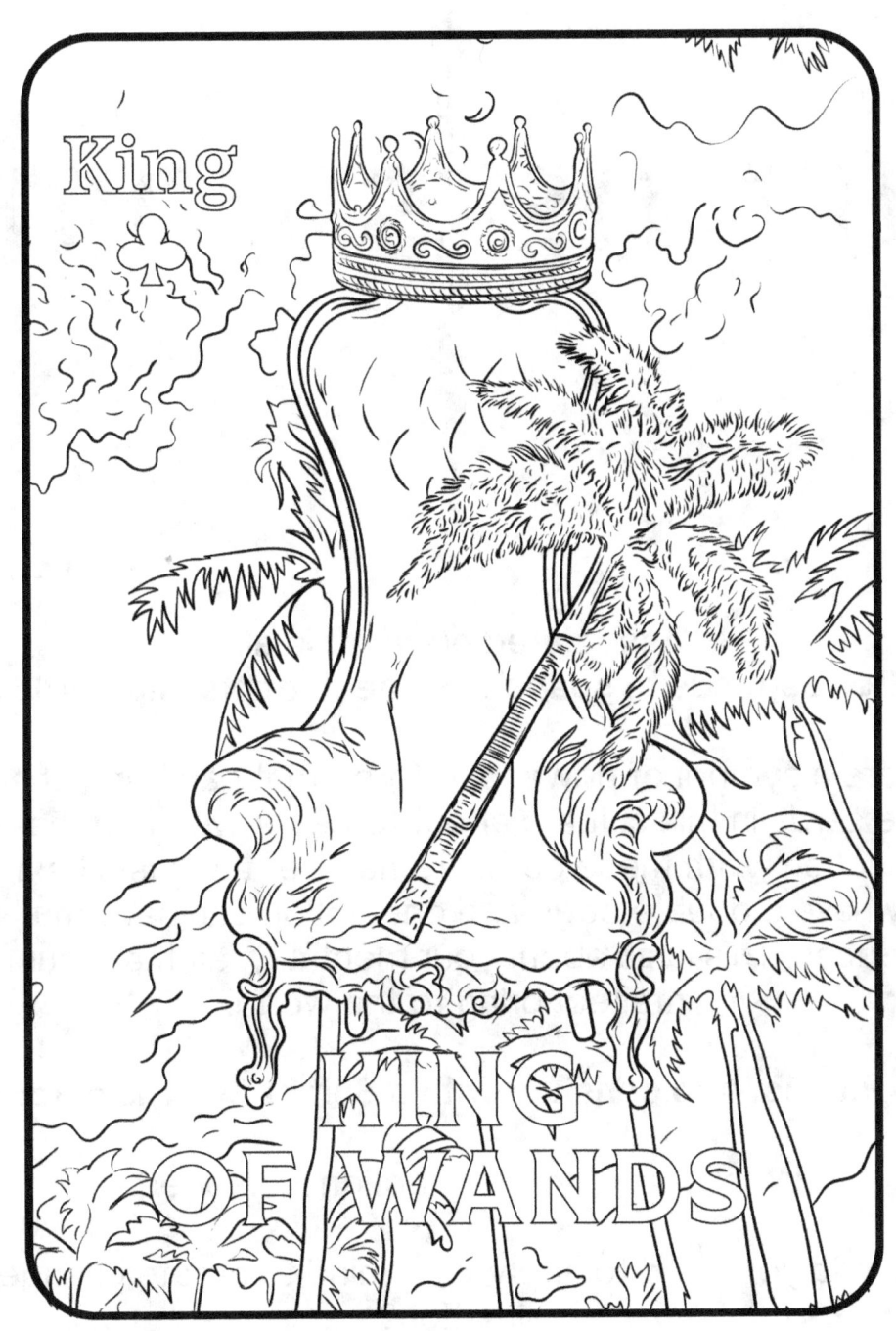

SUIT OF SWORDS

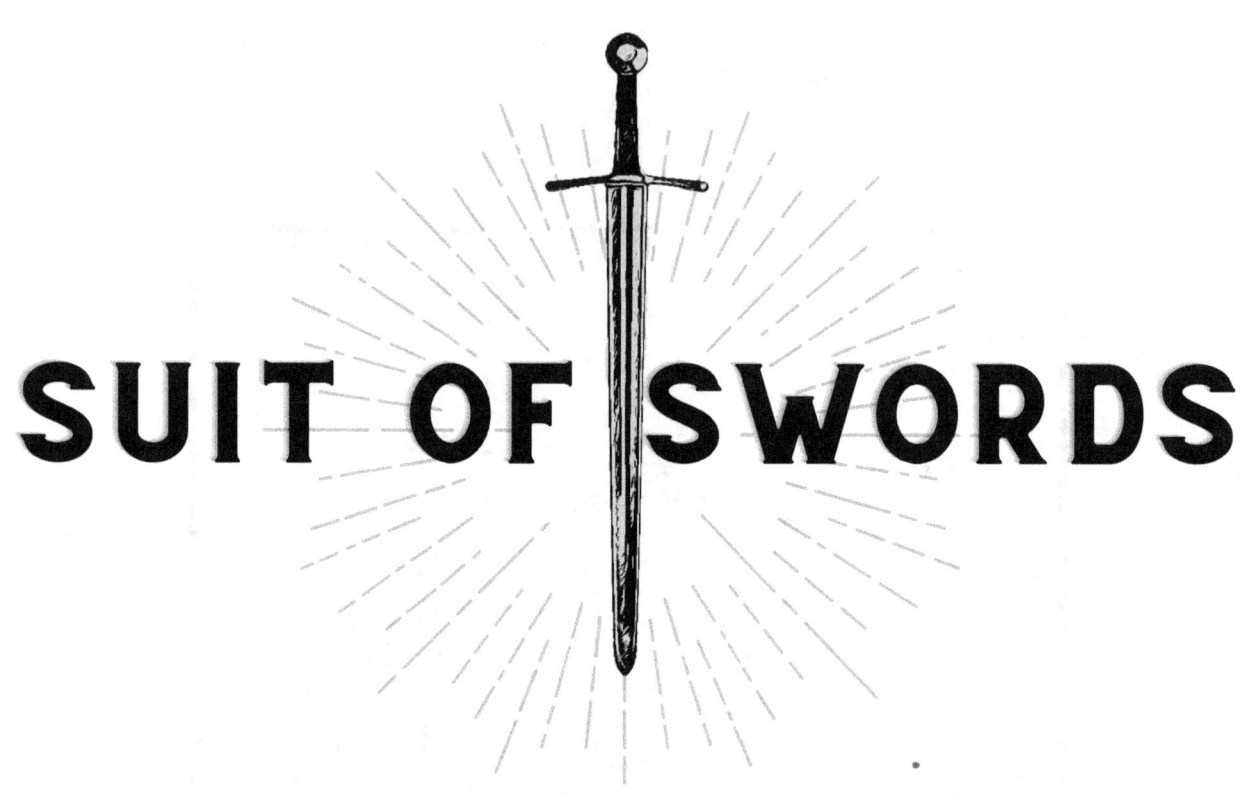

Associated element is air.
Corresponds to spades in a deck of playing cards

Swords are a symbol of power and force that can bring change to a land. The cards in this suit are about force, power, and the courage to take action. With these cards, remember that just like a sword, they have a double edge and one action can have multiple consequences. This is all about your mentality, all that your mind and intellect bring to the world.

Questions to consider with a Suit of Swords card:

What sort of force or action is needed?

Where do you need to apply your mind to create change in a situation?

What are both sides of an action you want to take?

SUIT OF SWORDS
QUICK GUIDE

Ace of Swords
Upright: Reasoning, sharpness of mind, and illuminating thought.

Reversed: Confusion, difficult times, and separation.

About the Wandering Traveler card: The view at Nu'uanu Pali State Park in Honolulu, Hawaii.

Two of Swords
Upright: Indecisions, stalemate, and blocked emotions and thoughts.

Reversed: No right choice, confusion, and indecision.

About the Wandering Traveler card: Hidden rocky cove in Honolulu, Hawaii.

Three of Swords
Upright: Heartbreak, grief, and rejection.

Reversed: Forgiveness, moving on, and recovery.

About the Wandering Traveler card: Rain on an office window in Seattle, Washington.

Four of Swords
Upright: Rest, recuperation, and contemplation.

Reversed: Burnt out, stress, and restlessness.

About the Wandering Traveler card: My meditation space in Coeur d'Alene, Idaho.

Five of Swords
Upright: Win at all cost, unchecked ambition, and betrayal.

Reversed: Forgiveness, past resentment, and open to change.

About the Wandering Traveler card: Leaving on a trip with my favorite travel bag in Coeur d'Alene, Idaho.
.

Six of Swords
Upright: Transition, moving on, and leaving the past behind.

Reversed: Unresolved issues, resisting life transitions, and carrying emotional baggage.

About the Wandering Traveler card: Manning the boat in Ilwaco, Washington.

SUIT OF SWORDS
QUICK GUIDE

Seven of Swords
Upright: Betrayal, trickery, and getting away with something.

Reversed: Telling the truth, breaking free, and rethinking plans.

About the Wandering Traveler card: Echo the Pomeranian is always watching so you'd better behave in Coeur d'Alene, Idaho.
.

Eight of Swords
Upright: Self-imposed restriction, imprisonment, and isolation.

Reversed: New perspective, freedom, and self-release.

About the Wandering Traveler card: The forest with a full moon rising in Spokane, Washington.

Nine of Swords
Upright: Nightmares, trauma, and depression.

Reversed: Reaching out, hope, and avoidance of negative manifestations.

About the Wandering Traveler card: Taking a nap with a squirrel-chasing nightmare in Snohomish, Washington.

Ten of Swords
Upright: Defeat, failure, and endings.

Reversed: Regeneration, the situation can't get worse, and inevitable end.

About the Wandering Traveler card: Finding a dead end while lost, somewhere near Waco, Texas.

Page of Swords
Upright: Restless energy, curiosity, and energetic.

Reversed: All talk, no action, not delivering on the agreement, and manipulation.

About the Wandering Traveler card: Turquoise skies of Belize.

Knight of Swords
Upright: Action-oriented, hasty, and defending thoughts and beliefs.

Reversed: Disregard for consequences, no direction, and scatterbrained.

About the Wandering Traveler card: Gate practice training in Ocala, Florida.

SUIT OF SWORDS
QUICK GUIDE

Queen of Swords
Upright: Perceptive, quick thinker, and independent.

Reversed: Cold-hearted, cruel, and callous.

About the Wandering Traveler card:
Some clouds in the sky at Venice Beach, California.

King of Swords
Upright: Intellectual power, truth, and authority.

Reversed: Manipulative, mentally abusive, and tyrant.

About the Wandering Traveler card:
The other half of the turquoise skies of Belize.

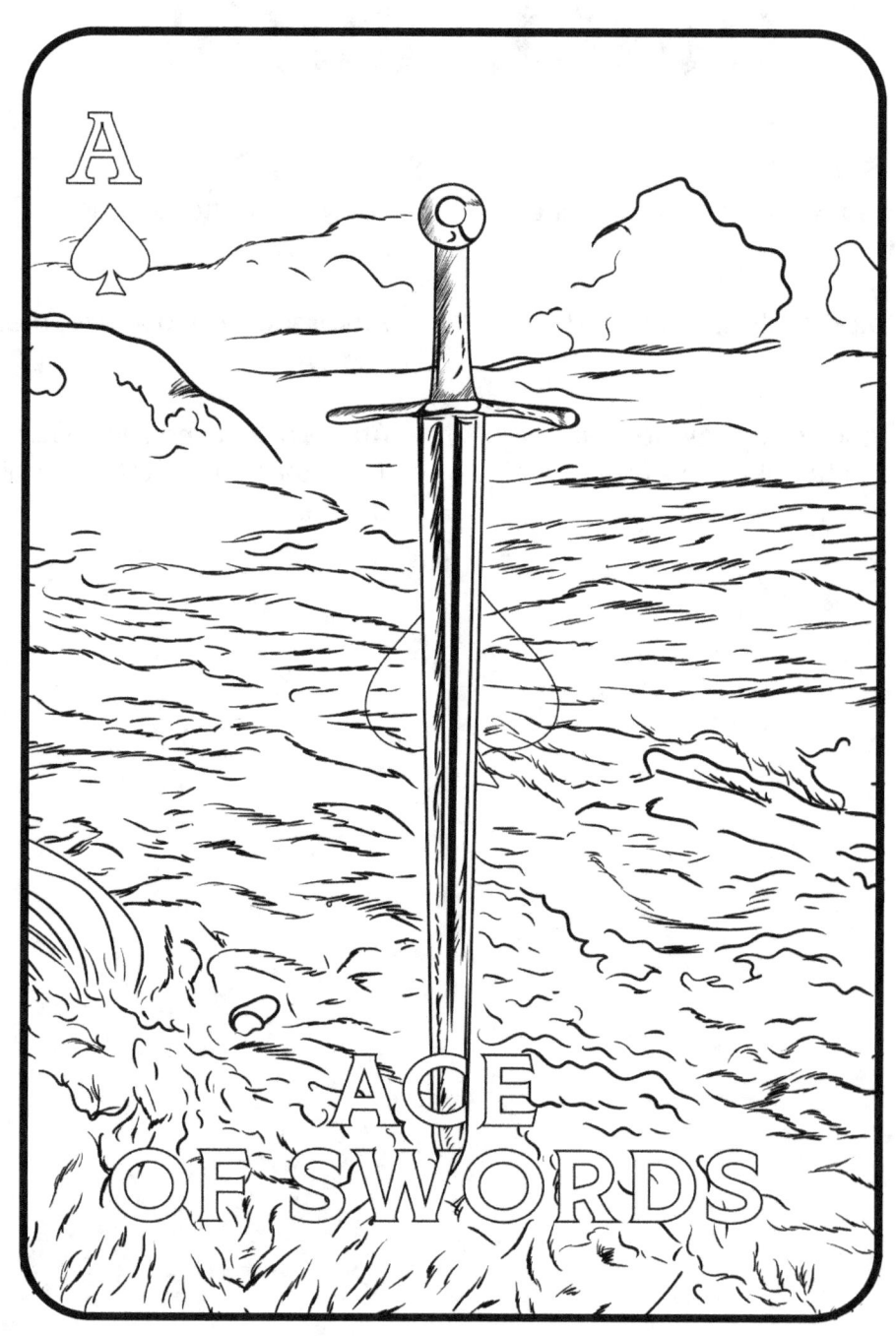

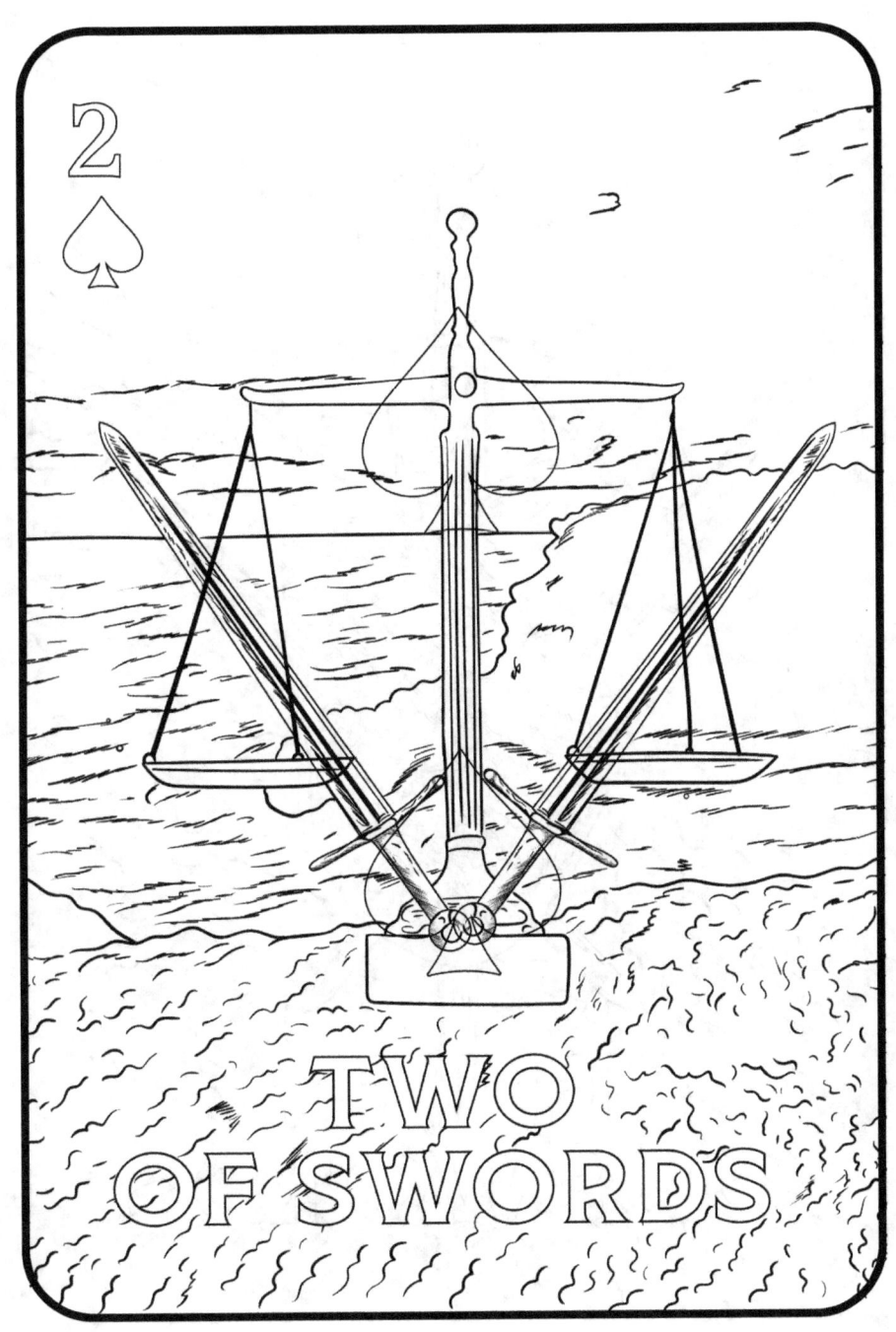

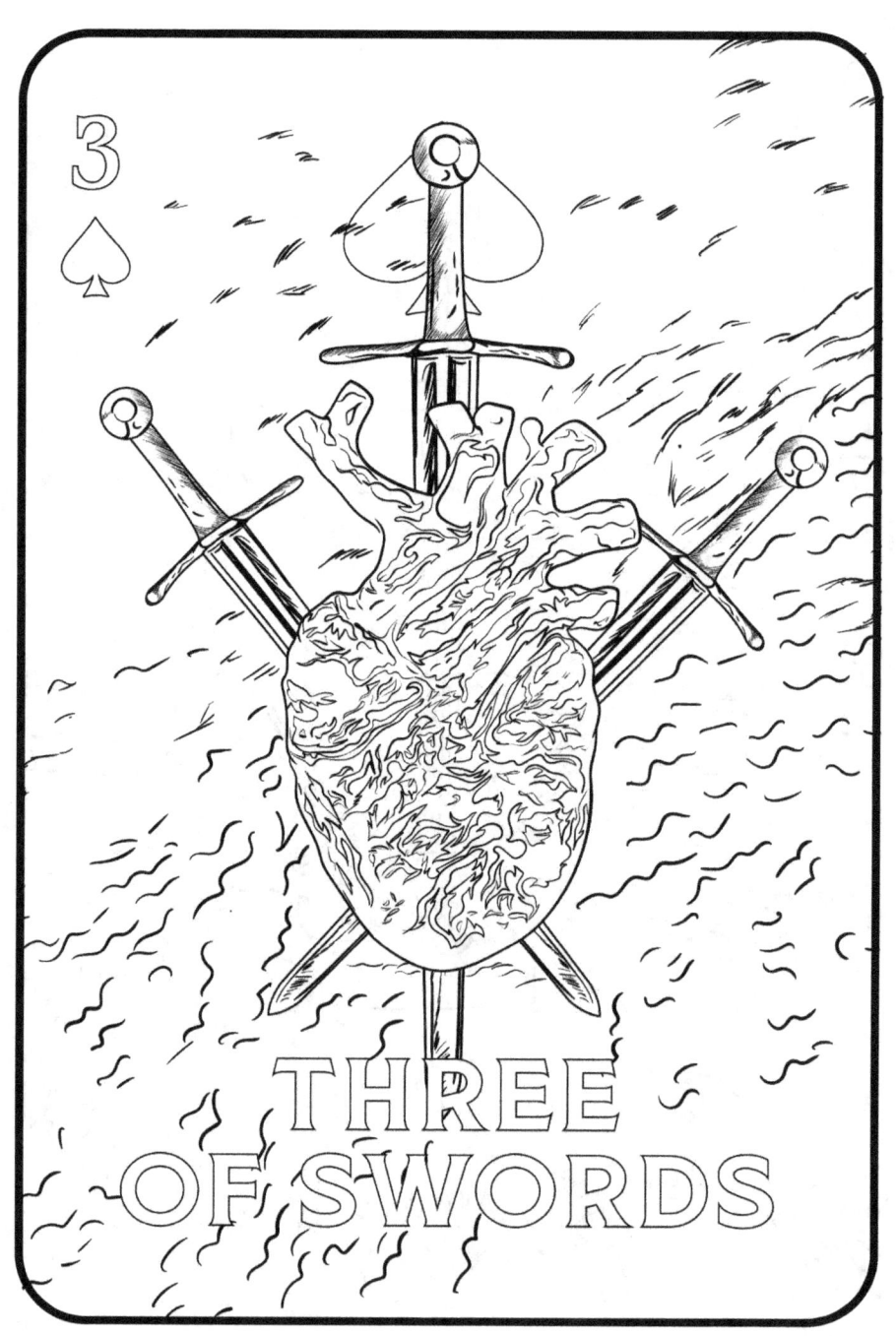

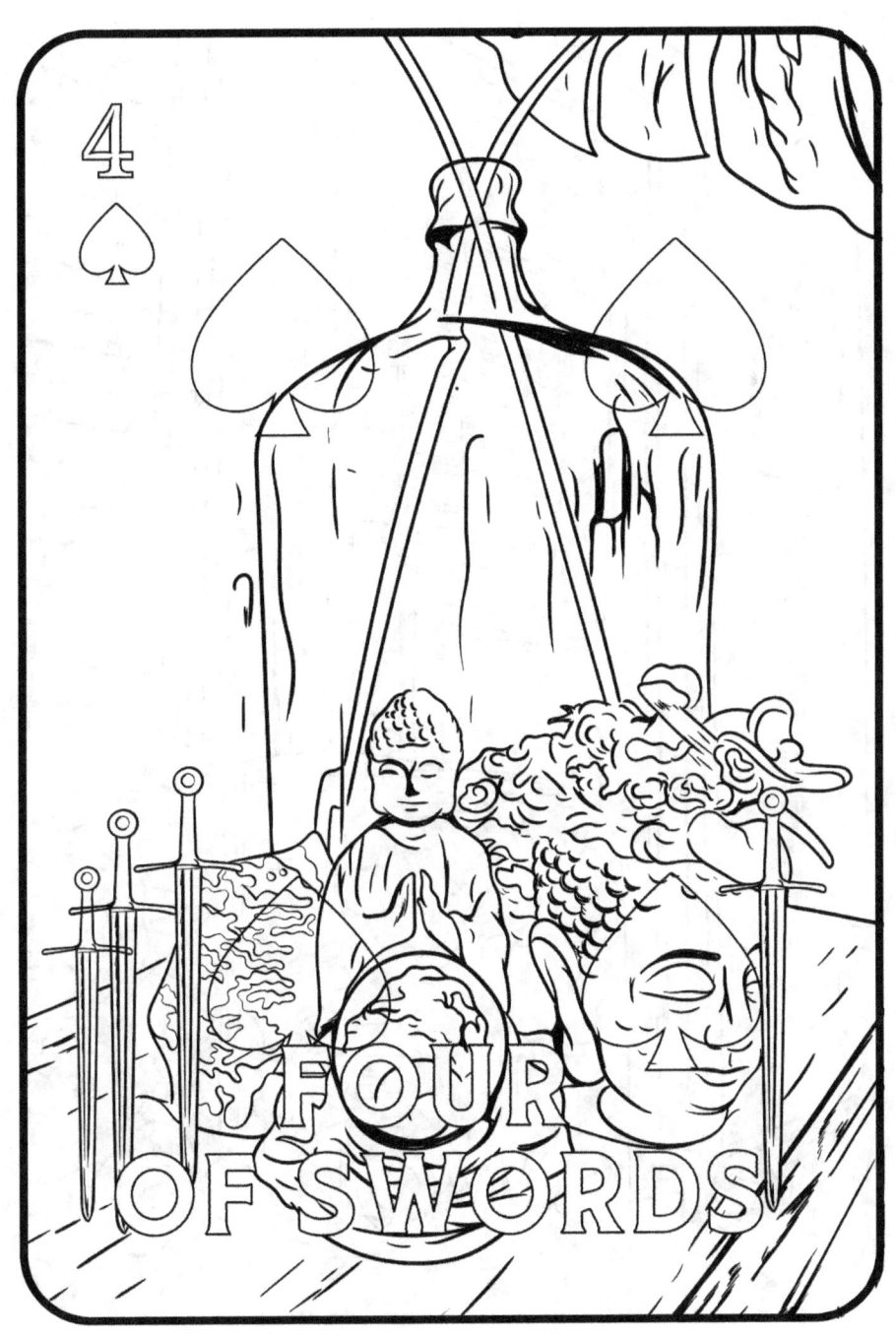

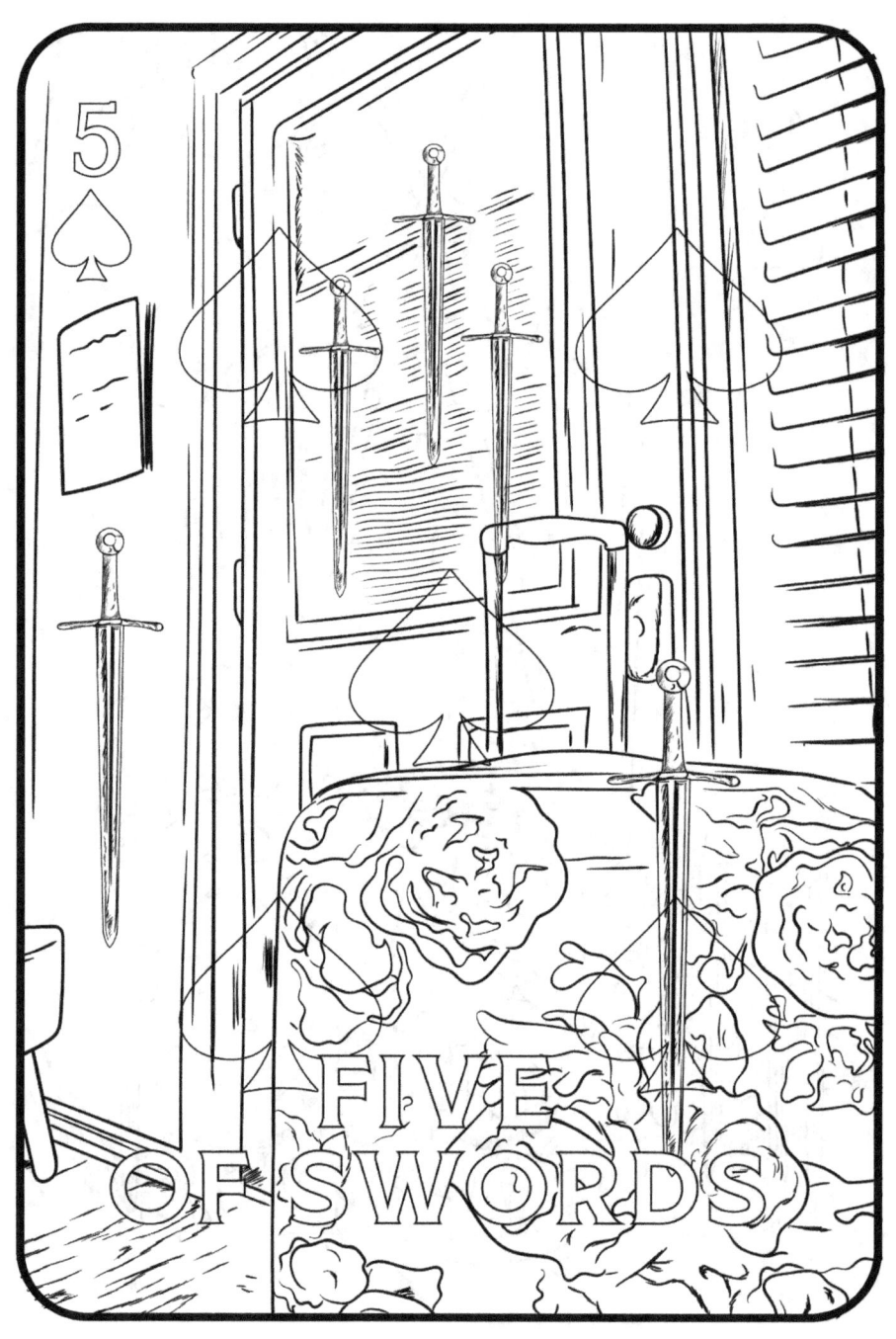

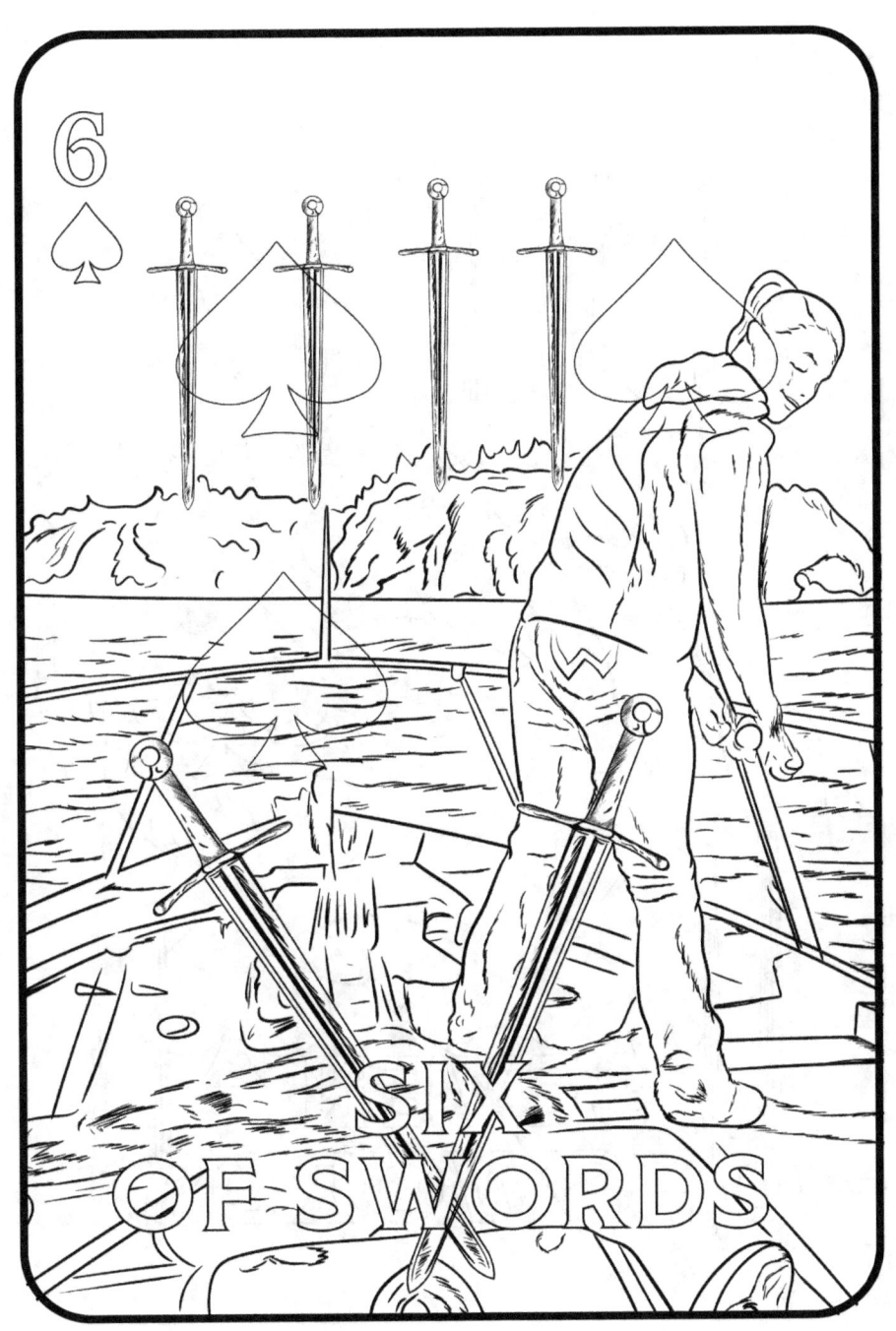

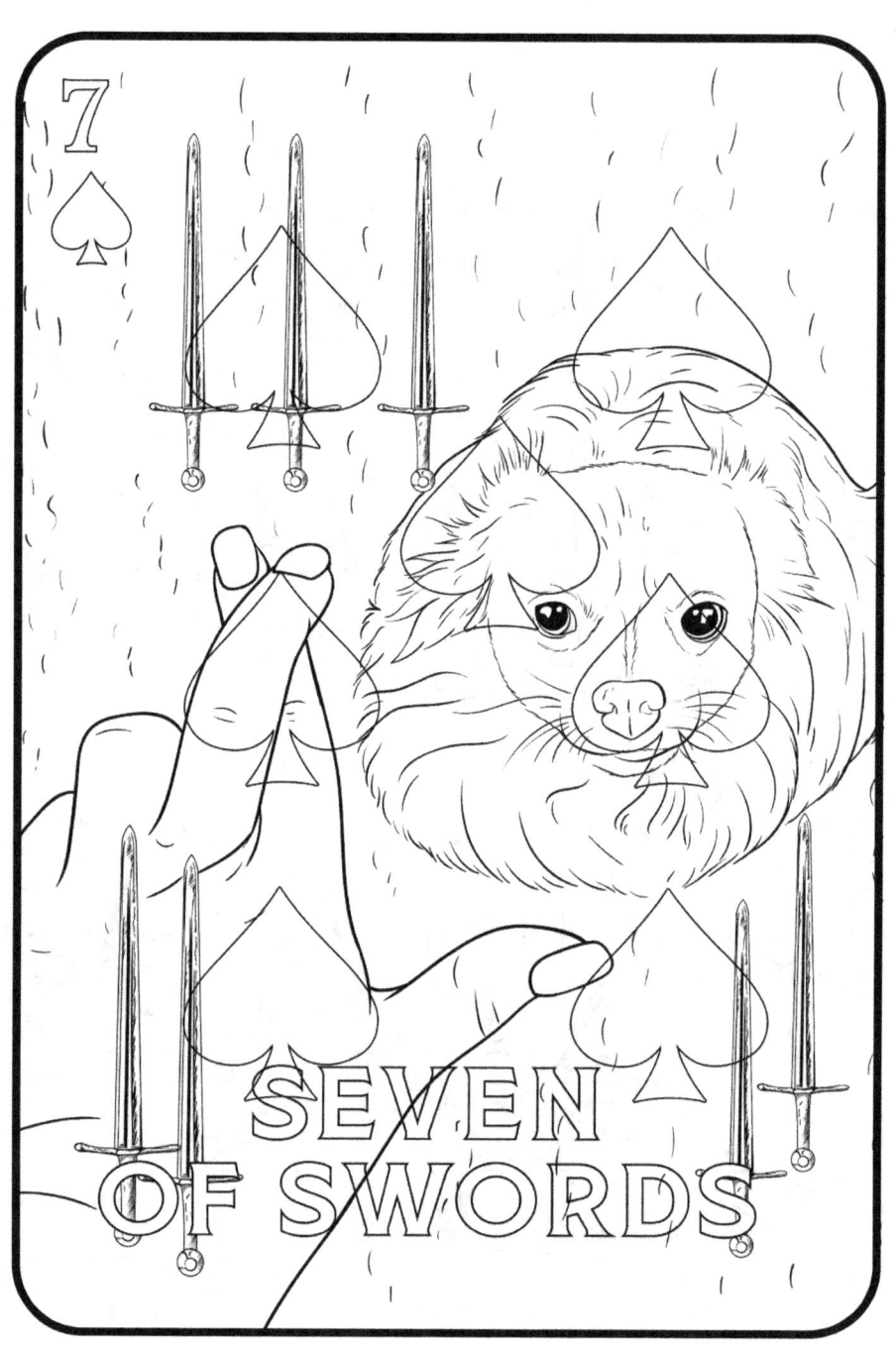

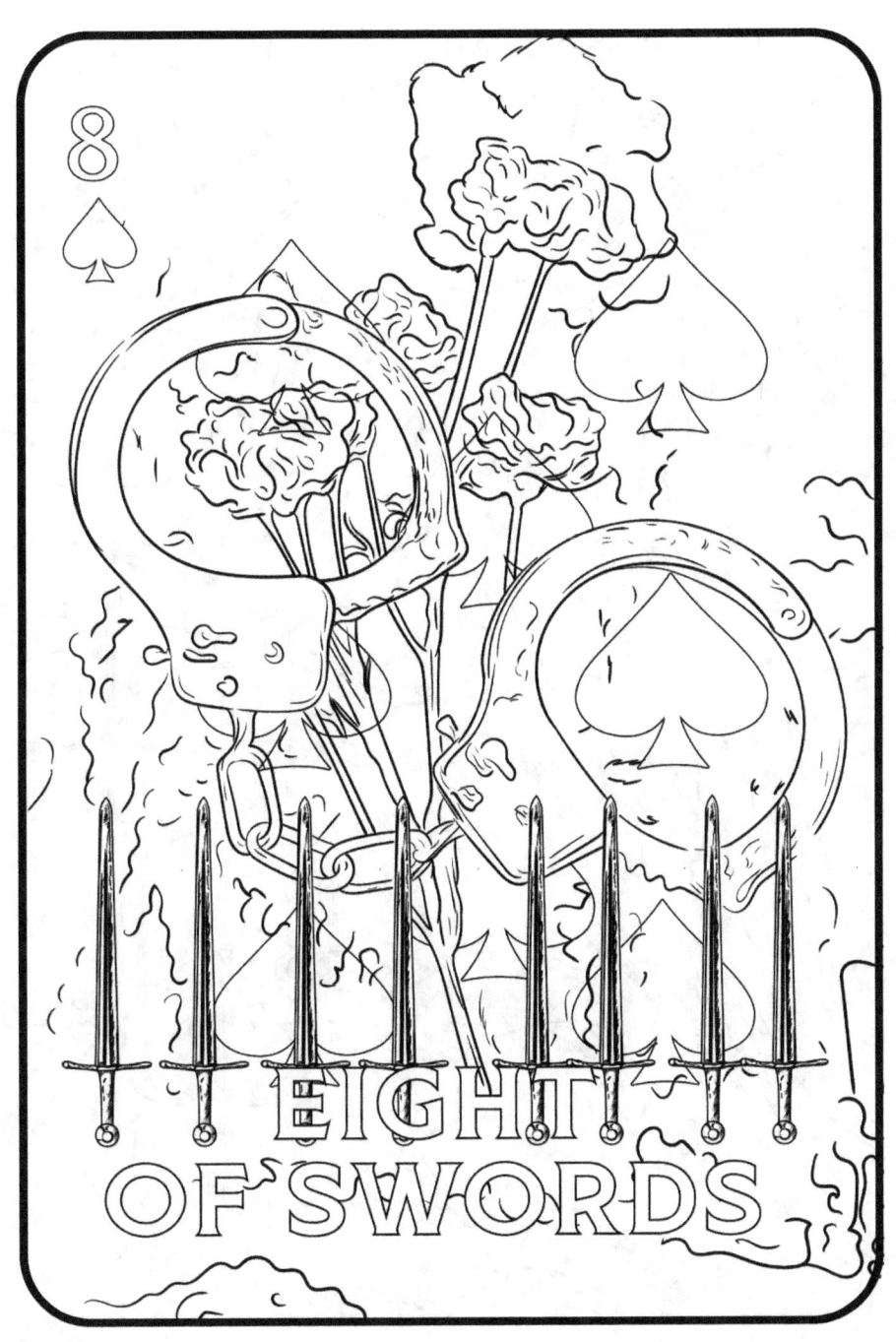

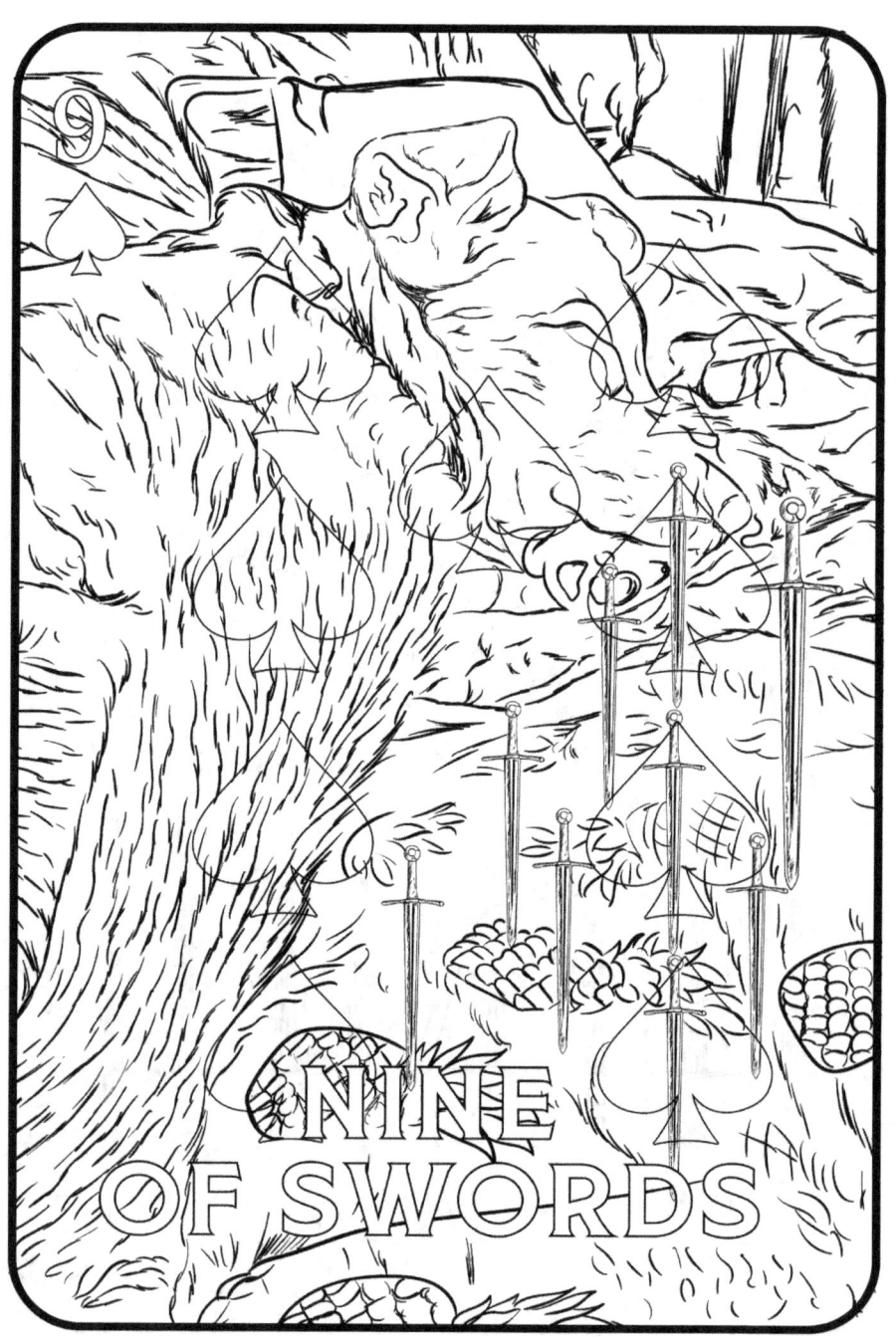

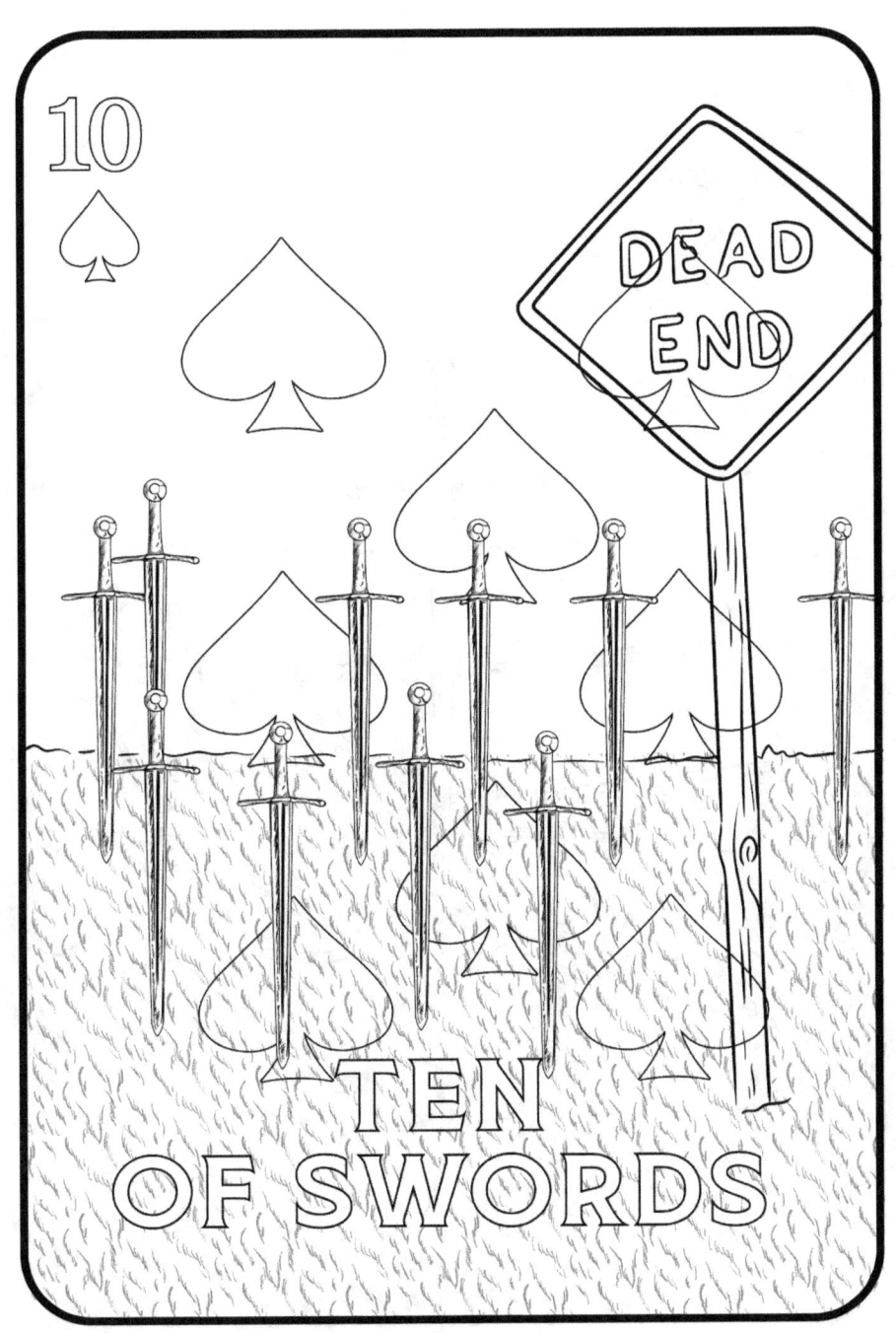

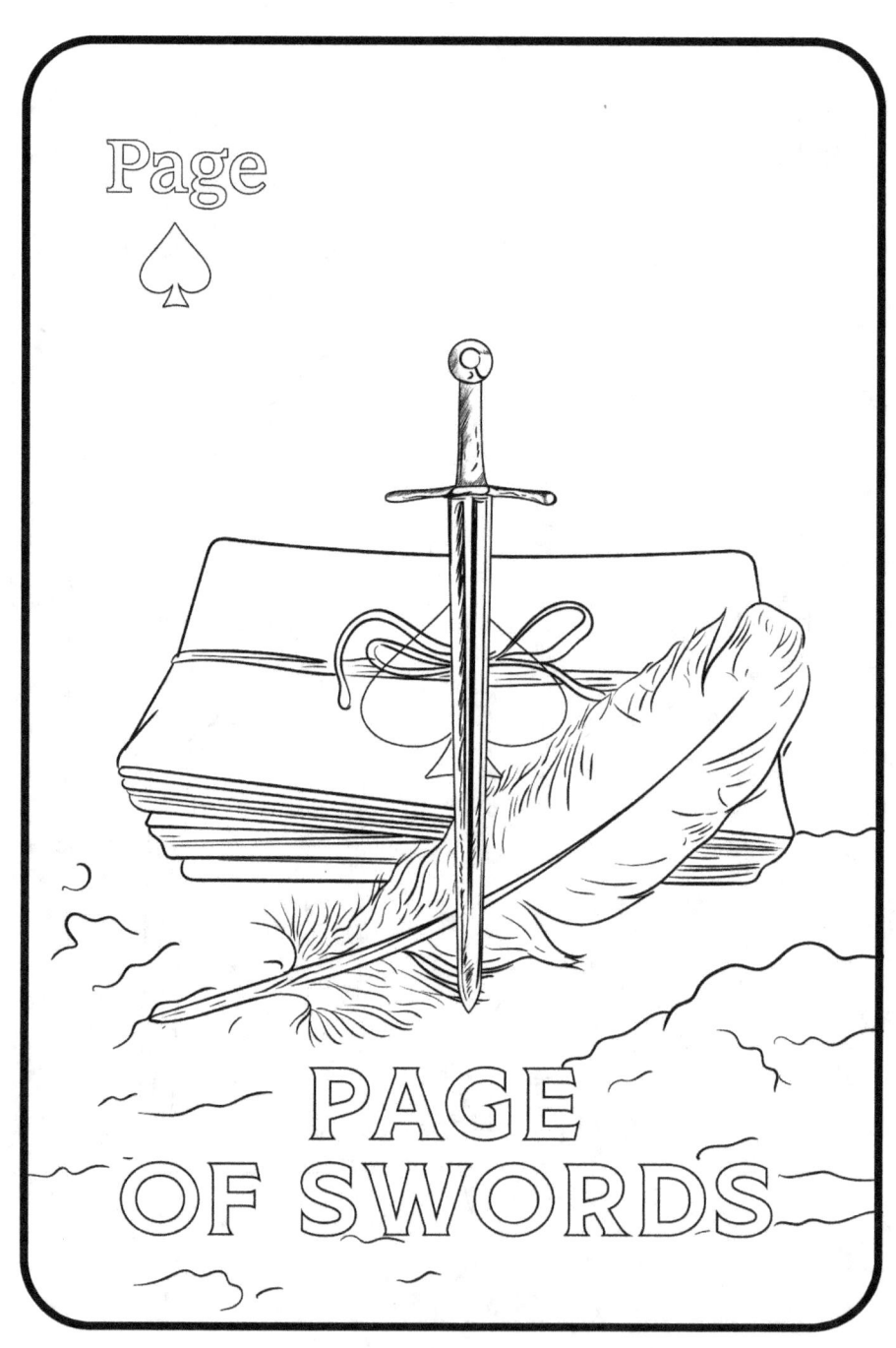

Page ♠

PAGE
OF SWORDS

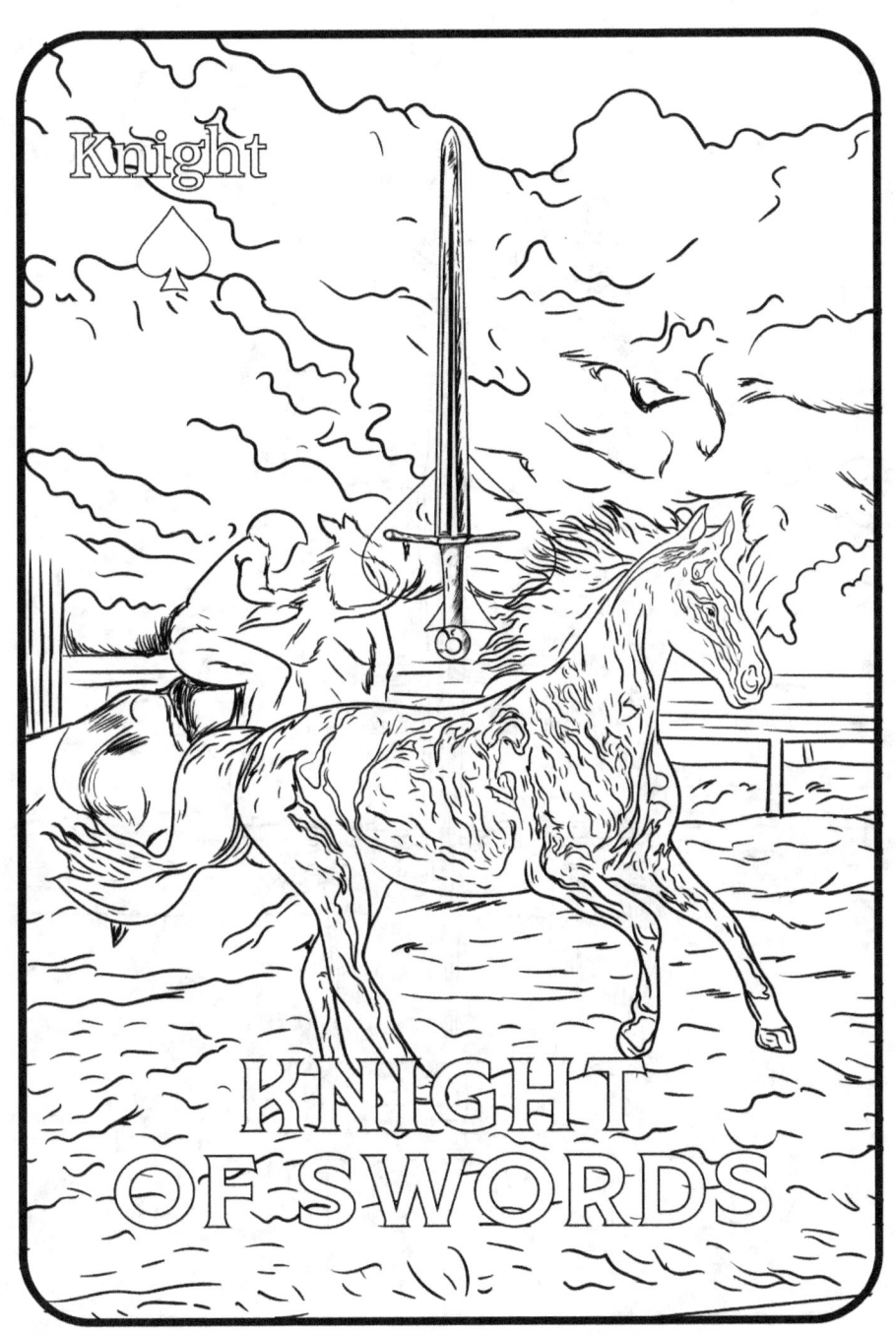

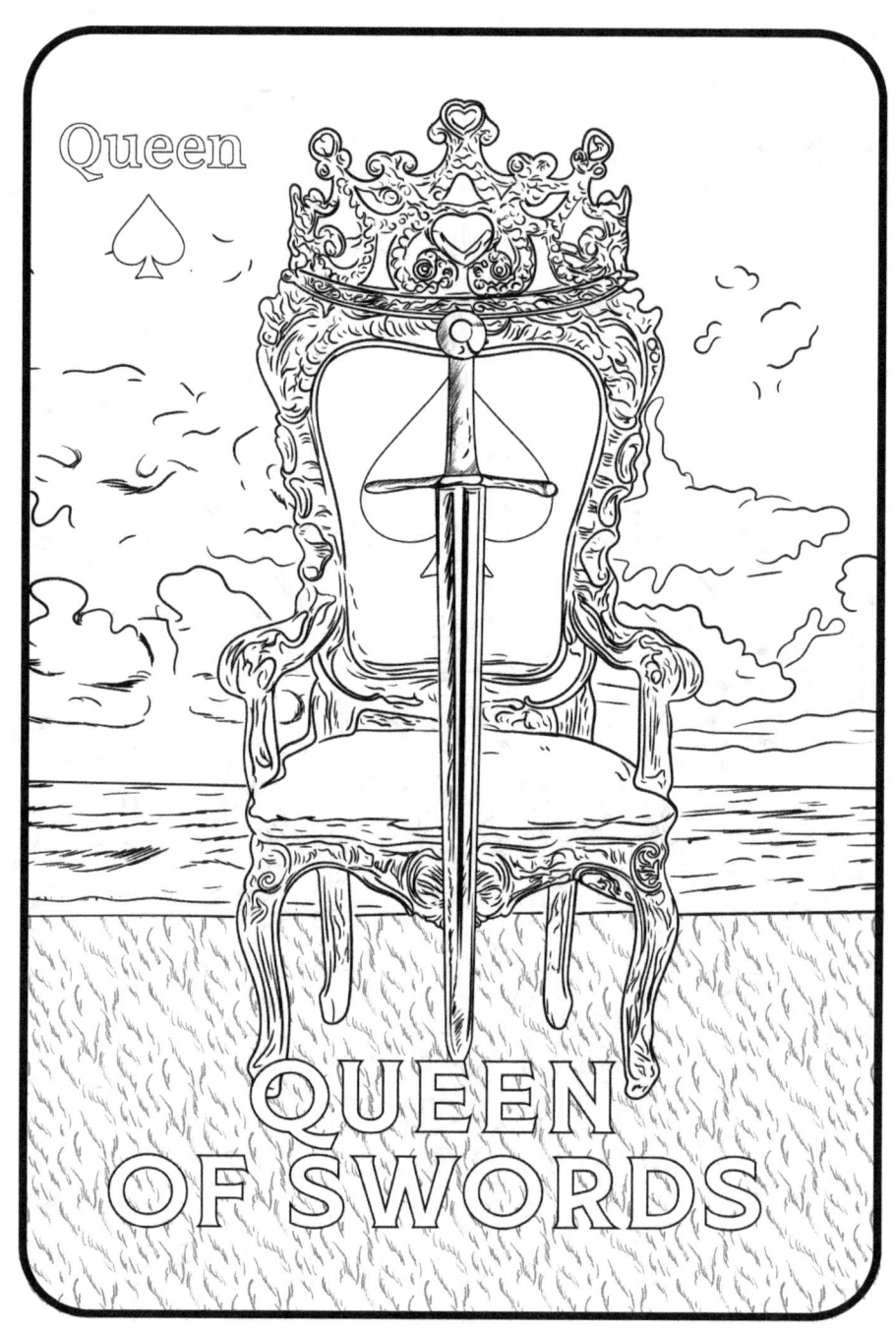

Queen

QUEEN
OF SWORDS

120

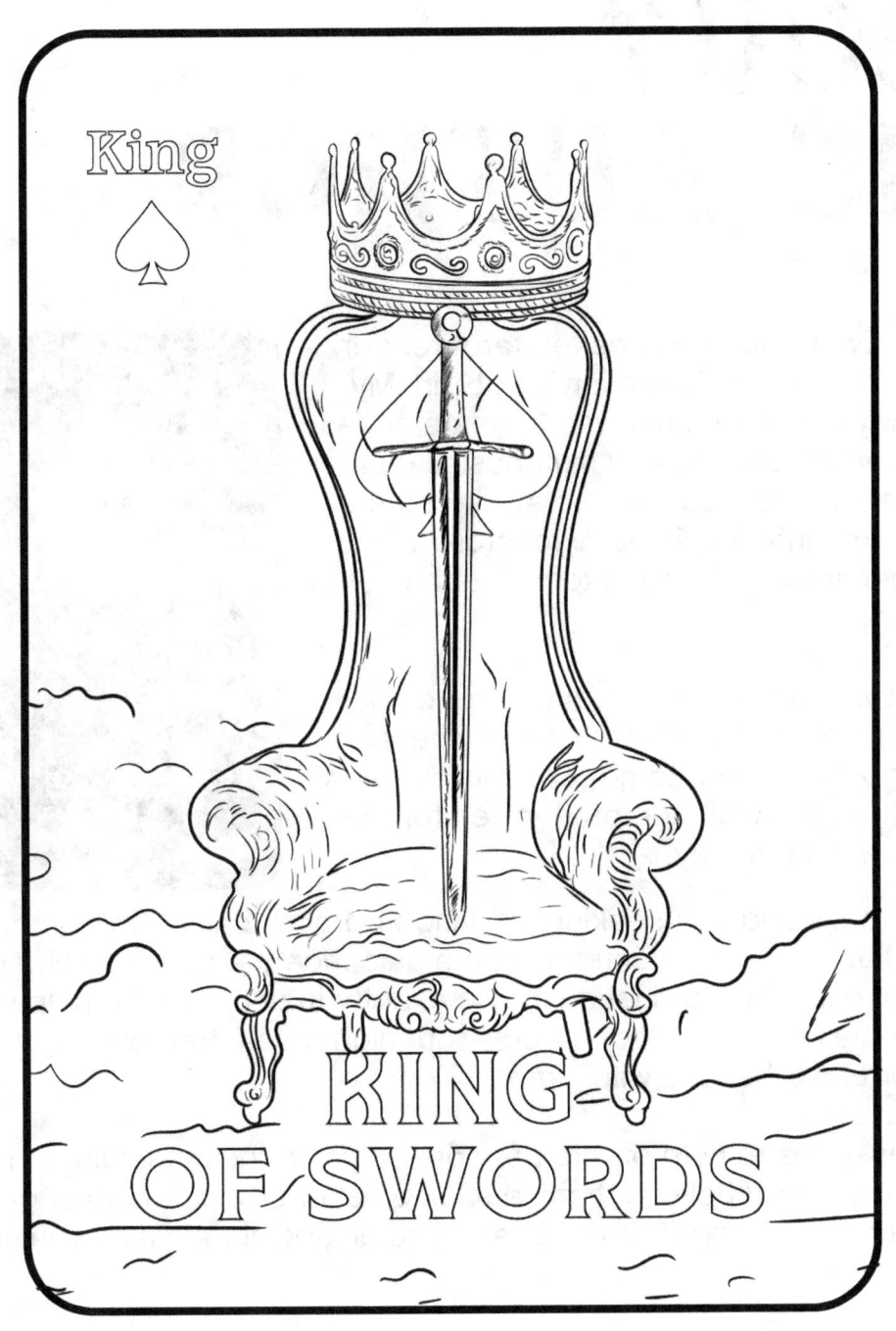

King

♠

KING
OF SWORDS

ABOUT THE AUTHOR

I'm Kendall Evans: author, speaker, tarot reader, and the creator of the Bohemian Tarot Girl. My Tarot journey started when I was 10 years old and my grandmother took me and my cousins on a trip to Vancouver, Canada. As we strolled the city, we walked into a spiritual bookstore. My grandmother allowed us each to pick out a set of tarot cards.

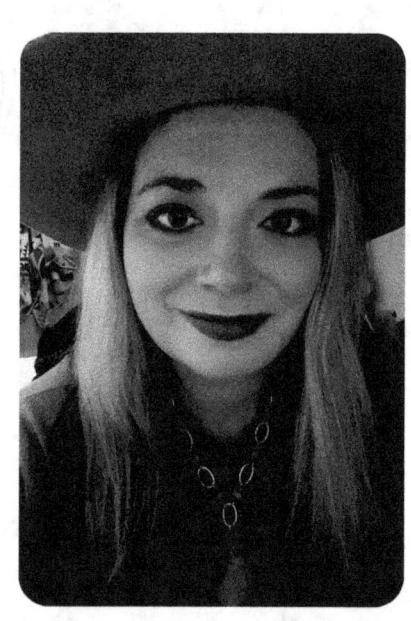

My first set was a mini Rider Waite Tarot deck and at that moment II had not realized what a powerful tool I'd chosen to get connected to my inner self. I thank my grandmother often for the gift she gave me that day.

I spent my teens and 20s seeking guidance from my cards. It was not until my early 30s that I made the connection: the guidance the cards provided was inside me already. This divination tool is exactly that: a "tool" to help us connect to the wisdom of the universe, our higher self. Remember, your soul is the best fortune teller you will find!

Now my passion is to help others get connected to the inner wisdom to which we all have access. I believe that we should never stop learning or growing while we are on this earth. I hope to see you on social media as you share your journey!

GET CONNECTED

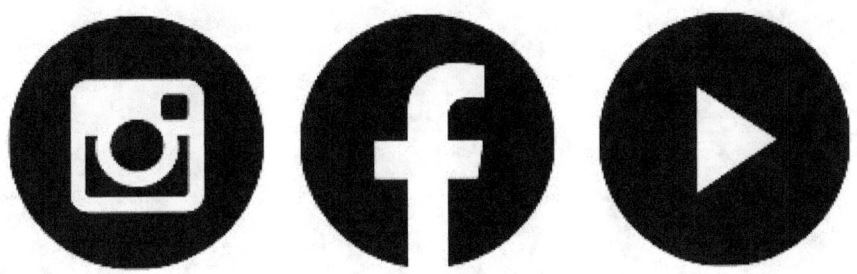

@BohemianTarotGirl
www.BohemianTarotGirl.com

Connect with the Author

www.KendallEvans.com

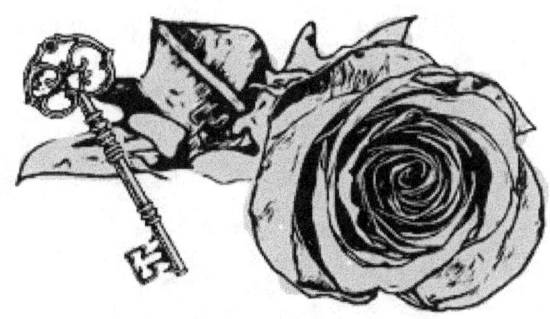